BOOK-KEEPING

THE
RIGHT WAY

BOOK-KEEPING

THE
RIGHT WAY

by

JOHN G. WHYTE-VENABLES

PAPERFRONTS
ELLIOT RIGHT WAY BOOKS
KINGSWOOD SURREY UK

Typeset in 10/11pt Times by County Typesetters,
Margate, Kent

Made and printed in Great Britain by Richard Clay Ltd.,
Bungay, Suffolk.

CONTENTS

Dedication

To my parents
and
Louise

Acknowledgements

Thanks are due to the following:

Anthony Halstead for reading and reviewing the text, and
Diana Quick for typing the manuscript.

1

Introduction

This book is intended for anyone who is starting a small business, or is involved in the running of a club or society, and needs to know how to keep financial records properly.

Keeping a track of money is essential to successful management of a small business or club. Unfortunately many cannot face the prospect of what they see as juggling "musty figures in dusty ledgers". The ability to handle numbers varies as widely between individuals as does any other talent. Some people are actually terrified of figure work and view the idea of book-keeping as a compound of boredom and masochism to be avoided at all costs. If you are one of them, take comfort. You are not alone.

The first thing to grasp is that book-keeping need not be difficult. You probably use more common sense and basic figurework in the pursuit of your craft or trade than you need to draw up a simple set of accounts. If you can manage straightforward addition and subtraction, then you will be able to keep track of your finances. If you apply multiplication and division you can, if shown how, produce a full set of accounts for which an accountant would charge you a great deal of money. Like many professionals, accountants have built up an intimidating vocabulary of their own, disguising the fundamental simplicity of the principles on which book-keeping works.

What is book-keeping?

Everybody who earns money has to account for it. The wage

earner has to pay tax to the government, whose collection agency is known as the Inland Revenue. The club treasurer is responsible for showing his governing committee that their funds are being spent wisely.

If you are employed in a job then the task of calculating tax is usually done by someone else. A pay clerk or similar official within the company will work out how much has been earned in a week or month, assess the tax payable to the government and pay the employees what is left. This system suits the employee, who does not have to worry about book-keeping. It suits the government because they are able to collect a lump sum from each company. On a nationwide scale it is obviously easier to collect tax from several thousand companies than twenty or thirty million employees!

A self-employed person works or trades as an individual. Whether he owns a small factory, or trades as a jobbing craftsman, he is basically working for himself, selling skills for a price, buying materials and generally supervising his own life. Keeping financial records, or "books" is part of the responsibility of being self-employed.

What does the government do about the self-employed?

The government recognises the self-employed person. It is a benefit of living in a free society that you are able to operate free of control from a higher authority in this way. It does mean, however, that you are responsible for your own finances. Once a year, an Income Tax Inspector will expect to see evidence of how much has been earned and will then calculate the amount of tax owed to the government. The Tax Inspector does however realise that a good deal of your income will have been spent in providing the goods or services which you, as a self-employed person, offer. He will therefore allow deduction of certain of these expenses from earnings before taxing the remainder.

It is, therefore, essential to record expenses, if only to minimise the amount of tax payable.

The books that the trader is required to keep are nothing more than a record of what was earned and what has been spent. This record is usually compiled in one book, a CASH BOOK, which is kept up to date on a daily, weekly or monthly basis. A small business can quite often function with this one record. Do not be put off book-keeping by the thought of having to keep an endless series of incomprehensible ledgers. They will not be necessary – at least until the concern grows to considerable size.

At the end of the year accounts can (but in some cases need not) be prepared. Accounts are nothing more than a summary of the financial affairs of the business for a given period, usually a year. Whether you are a self-employed craftsman, a housewife, or a club treasurer, you will realise that money really only does two things: it comes in, or it goes out. A simple set of accounts merely summarises on a few sheets of paper where your business income came from and where it went during the year. As you work through this book you will meet terms such as "profit and loss account" and "balance sheet". Do not panic! They are just different ways of expressing where money comes from and where it goes.

Who are the self-employed?

A self-employed person is anyone who trades as an individual, choosing the jobs he or she wishes to do and taking the responsibility for their completion.

People become self-employed for a number of reasons. A prime cause at the time of writing is redundancy. Finding yourself without a job, possibly after many years' service, can be deeply upsetting. You may seek another job in the same field but without success. Competition for posts may rise and jobs themselves disappear as men are superseded by machines, or entire processes replaced by new technology.

Nevertheless you might still be able to apply your skills, this time working for yourself.

A second reason involves career progression. In some areas, including engineering, architecture and other professions, the possibility of becoming a consultant may offer itself. Or you may just enjoy the prospects of being your own boss!

Thirdly, there are those whose work involves self-employment from the start – for instance, musicians, artists, craftsmen and writers. In some creative fields no career structure does or could exist. People in these occupations will consider self-employment as soon as they start work.

There are also the partially self-employed. An example might be the factory worker who plays in a band in the evenings. Anyone, in fact, who has a paying hobby and who ought to declare the income.

In all these examples, self-employment offers the opportunity of being your own boss and doing what you are best at according to your own rules. The other side of the coin is that you are responsible for your own fate. There will no longer be a buffer between you and officialdom. There will be a direct accountability for tax. Suppliers will want their bills paid, cheerfully ignoring protests that you have not been paid yourself. Machines may break down at crucial moments.

A good working knowledge of how to keep financial records can help to forestall some of these problems. Too many small businesses go to the wall because their owners were competent at the work bench or easel, or on the building site, but were bemused by the paper work.

Who needs to see accounts?

There are three people who will want to see the records of a business. The first is the Tax Inspector, unless you are merely preparing accounts for a club or society. A self-employed person is responsible for his or her financial affairs, so the Tax Inspector will require records to be kept of the money earned so that he can estimate how much tax, if any, is payable. It is not strictly necessary to prepare a set of accounts for the Inland Revenue; you do not *need* to summarise records at the end of the year, it is acceptable to show the Inspector your day-to-day records from which he will then draw up his own accounts. He will, however, appreciate a neatly kept and accurate record of income and expenditure connected with the business. If he can assess the tax position of the business quickly and easily, it will take him less time to confirm the accuracy of the figures, and may well avoid the necessity for awkward and time-consuming correspondence over queries. The record is also your own check of the accuracy of his calculations!

The second person to be interested in the financial affairs of a business is the bank manager.

There is no legal requirement to submit records to the bank. However, if a bank loan is needed, or an overdraft facility or advice on money matters generally, the bank manager will want to see how well or how badly the business is doing. If he is shown well-kept records which demonstrate that you are in control of your finances, the bank manager is more likely to offer a friendly ear.

The third person interested in financial records is you, the businessman. If records are kept along the lines given in this book, you will find it much easier to manage the business properly. For instance, it is possible to assess whether additional sales are needed in a particular month.

If a van is required in order to distribute wares, an intelligent study of the cash book will allow prediction of the best time to buy.

These decisions can be made anyway, but without cash flow information they would be haphazard, and there would always be the nagging doubt as to whether the decision was sound.

The club or association treasurer

The treasurer or book-keeper will find the position more straightforward. We will be discussing club accounting in detail later (see page 102) but mention now that the role of club treasurer is to keep an accurate record of the income and expenditure of the club. The prospective treasurer will have been offered the post or elected to it, as the committee member in charge of the club's financial affairs. It is therefore the ruling committee of the club who will want to be kept informed of progress in order to be able to budget ahead. The members will need the figures at the A.G.M. to see how their money has been spent and received.

Who are accountants?

The accountant who hangs up his brass plate in the High Street is a highly trained tax and accountancy expert who makes his living by compiling accounts and sometimes day-to-day records for clients and then liaising with the Tax Inspector on their behalf.

If a solicitor is already retained to deal with legal affairs, you might ask, "Why should I bother to keep independent records when it is possible to employ an accountant?"

Taking advice from a professional accountant can be expensive. He has to cover all his costs and overheads, such as staff and premises and spreads these expenses amongst his clients. This means that you may be charged a substantial sum for every hour spent by the accountant and his clerks in processing your accounts. The bill for the compilation of a set of accounts will be considerable. Yet much of the work of preparing these accounts is done by the clerks, using techniques based on simple principles such as these given in this book.

Another factor to consider is loss of financial control. Of course you can consign the task of book-keeping to a professional accountant at the end of each year. But then it is not possible to have the day-to-day knowledge of cash movements which you need for informed business management. An accountant could provide regular reports if asked, but this would be very expensive.

Solicitors and accountants differ in the extent to which you could perform their tasks yourself. It would need considerable dedication to learn sufficient law to make significant saving on legal costs. To maintain accounting records, however, is rather easier, given practice and guidance. The more you do yourself, the less you need to pay for expensive professional help.

The private individual, with simple book-keeping requirements, can safely forego the luxury of an accountant – certainly as regards keeping day-to-day records of business.

There are two circumstances when it is necessary or wise to consult an accountant.

Firstly, complex tax affairs are beyond the abilities of an amateur. For instance, investments, pensions and trusts all require professional management. Here skilled advice is money well spent.

Secondly, you need to consult an accountant if and when a *limited company* is formed. Whether or not a business is "limited" is indicated in the U.K. by the letters Ltd. after the company name. The technical term is "limited liability" company. A limited liability company is a distinct legal entity, able to enter into contracts in its own right. The owners become employees of the company, and sign "for and on behalf of" the company. One aspect of limited status is that the owners are not personally liable for debts incurred by the company, unless they volunteer liability by guaranteeing debts personally. This can be an important advantage to the small businessman. The drawback to running a limited company is that the law requires a qualified accountant to *audit*, or check, the truth of the company's financial records. The trader can still prepare his own records, and even the accounts which summarise them at the end of the year, but a professional accountant must check and sign them.

The eleventh Commandment

I include here a word of advice on "adjusting records" to show false figures. Although there are grounds to believe this practice is widespread, do not be tempted. The Tax Inspector is a wily and experienced professional who will soon spot efforts to gild the lily. The risk is unnecessary. As will be seen in the rest of the book there are a great many legitimate expenses that can be claimed against profits before there is a need to pay tax. There is often more to gain by claiming all possible allowances than from doctoring the records.

How to use this book

The important thing is not to panic and assume that you have no head for figures. The guidelines are not difficult. Just work through the chapters carefully and you should quickly understand them. As you apply them you will realise that five minutes of practice is worth an hour of reading.

2

Organising an office

Let us start by planning the office. This can be large or small according to the means and the facilities available. The important thing is that there is somewhere to work and somewhere to store records.

People vary in their approach to paperwork. Some tackle the task in a methodical and tidy manner with notes of each project kept each in its own file in a particular box or drawer. At any one time, they know exactly where to put their hands on a particular item. Others work differently. No matter how neat their initial system, filing systems soon degenerate into a slovenly pile with folders and correspondence distributed liberally over every available worktop, including the floor. The remarkable thing about the latter system is that it may work – for the individual concerned! Providing nothing is moved by an outsider he or she will still be able to find things. The rule here is to follow personal inclination. Do not worry if you cannot work in a clinical fashion. It is best if you are happy with your own particular system.

The basic office

The simplest requirements for an office are a corner to work in, something to work on, and somewhere to put things. Depending on your circumstances this can be a purpose-built office in a factory, or the dining room table. If you are fortunate enough to have a separate office, all records can be stored there. If you resort to a work bench corner or the family table, you need to think about a portable storage system in order to avert the wrath of the next user of the table.

If you need to concentrate for some time, then you want peace and quiet, good lighting and adequate warmth. The task of up-dating records accurately is considerably more tedious if you work in a freezing out-house under poor light!

The desk

Any worktop will serve if it is convenient and comfortable. If you can afford a proper desk, so much the better. It should measure 2'3" to 2'6" high and be fitted with at least one, preferably two, large drawers. The desk top should be as big as possible to give you room to spread yourself. It is tiresome to squeeze into too small a space. The desk should be firm and stable, especially if you, or perhaps a secretary, will be pounding away at a typewriter.

Shops specialising in office equipment market a wide range of suitable desks. These can be expensive however, and it is worth scanning the classified advertisements in your local paper for a secondhand example.

If you do buy a secondhand desk, there are one or two points to watch. Check the joints to see that they are strong. Make sure that the drawers are big enough for your requirements and that you are given the keys to them if they are lockable. Watch out for woodworm – check the drawers for this as well.

The chair

Almost any chair will serve for the office, even a kitchen stool – that is, unless your trade requires that you entertain clients from the same chair. You may spend some hours every month at the desk, so for comfort it is best to find a well-built example with a strong back. You may well find a good one second-hand, or even on a market stall. Before you buy it, make sure it will fit the desk.

Lighting

When you are poring over figures, the last thing you want is poor lighting. If the general room illumination is inadequate, borrow or buy a desk lamp. Anglepoise lights which can be adjusted are the best bet. If you intend to do much typing, you want the light to shine onto the paper and not into your eyes.

Fig. 1   Layout of office

Shelves and storage

You could keep your files in your desk drawers but it is better
to label the files and store them on shelves where they can be
seen. You can then use the desk drawers for stationery. If one
of the drawers is lockable, use it for confidential files, such as
those containing bank statements and other material which
you would prefer kept from prying eyes.

An ideal small office suitable for the corner of a workshop
or home is shown in Fig. 1.

Calculators and adding machines

For most small businesses an electronic calculator is suitable
and can be obtained very cheaply in the High Street. There is
no need for a sophisticated model; a calculator offering
addition, subtraction, multiplication and division will be quite
adequate.

If the business is larger and you have to add long lists of
numbers, it is worth buying an adding machine. This is a desk
machine which works like a calculator but with the advantage
that the numbers are printed onto a roll of paper. The roll is
useful to check that figures have been entered correctly. It
also forms a permanent record of calculations for later
reference.

Electronic adding machines are freely available.

Typewriter

A typewriter is practically essential. A clearly legible letter or
invoice will impress clients.

There is no need to invest in an expensive model. Reliable
second-hand machines are widely available.

If you are able to afford it, you can employ a part-time
secretary, but there is no reason why you should not handle
your own correspondence, at least at first. Nor is it necessary
to be able to type properly. With practice, proficiency with
two fingers can soon be gained and speeds of thirty words a

minute are quite practical. Learning to type properly is not impossible. There are several good tutors on the market but the process does demand time, which you probably do not have.

Stationery

You will need to equip yourself with a number of files and books to maintain the records. These can be bought from office stationers, or you can design and produce your own. These will save money and can be tailored to suit your own requirements.

It is worth considering having your own business stationery printed professionally. Your business image may be enhanced if your invoices and letter-heads are embossed with your trading name and logo. Any jobbing printer will quote you for the work.

The following essential items should be acquired before you start trading:

Invoice book
Order book
Cash book

Equip yourself with a selection of pencils, ball-point pens and notepaper. You may also need typewriter paper and liquid eraser. Loose-leaf files are useful for keeping copies of letters, invoices and orders.

3

Keeping a record

There are two distinct types of paperwork needed in running a business.

The first relates to selling goods and ordering materials. That is, the means by which you communicate with suppliers and customers.

The second is internal paperwork, keeping a record of money earned and spent which builds up into a picture of your financial affairs. These internal records will eventually form the basis of your accounts.

Basic business procedure

The first step in selling a product or service is to advertise it, whether by word of mouth, press or otherwise. Stall-holders and shop-keepers rely mainly on the display of their wares to attract custom.

From the moment that you attract an interested customer you must communicate with him in business terms.

For the shop-keeper, the transaction is brief and the negotiating is done by word of mouth. A shop-keeper's goods are generally on display with a note of the price. The customer will tell you he wishes to buy an item and money changes hands. For this money you may or may not be required to give a *receipt*. This is simply a brief note of what the customer bought and how much he spent. Receipts are commonly given for expensive goods (as they act as proof of purchase should the customer return with a query) but not for cheap items. From a book-keeping point of view you need to record the money you received from customers, but there is no paperwork involved in the actual transaction with the customer.

If, however, you offer a service or produce goods to order, then you will be *commissioned* to work for someone. An artist may be asked to execute a portrait or a small engineering company might be required to produce a number of components

First you will be approached by the client and asked for a *quote*. The price that you quote for the work will determine whether your customer employs you. Guidance on how to calculate a realistic price is given on page 24. Quotes are best phrased in the style of Fig. 2 if they are given by letter. If you discuss the commission verbally then it is essential to ensure that both you and the customer are absolutely clear about what you are quoting for.

J. BROWN – CARPENTER

(address and phone number)

(Date)

A. Smith, Esq.
(address)

Dear Mr. Smith,
   Thank you for your enquiry regarding the manufacture of a bedside cabinet.
   I am pleased to quote for the work as follows:
   To produce one pine bedside cabinet with two drawers   400
   Delivery charges   25
                                                        ─────
                                                        £425

   Your order will be completed by (date).

                        Yours sincerely

Fig. 2   A sample quote

If the price that you quote is satisfactory, then the customer will place an *order* with you (Fig. 3). The details of the order should be recorded in your order book. This will remind you of what the customer requires and act also as a source of reference if there is a dispute about the order.

A. SMITH
(address and phone number)

(Date)

J. Brown, Esq.
(address)

Dear Mr. Brown,
　Please supply:
　One off bedside cabinet in pine, with two drawers.
　The quoted price of £400 plus delivery charges of £25 is satisfactory.
　Delivery is anticipated in *(x weeks)*.

　　　Yours sincerely

　　　(signed)

　　　A. SMITH

Fig. 3   A sample order

At this stage, work on the commission can be started.
Once the work is finished you will need to be paid. It is possible that the customer will pay you in person. This may be similar to the case of the shop-keeper. The customer will check the work done and then pay either in cash or by cheque. If required, you can give him or her a receipt to conclude the deal.
The more formal way to request payment is by what is known as "raising an *invoice*". An invoice is commonly

known as a bill. This is a statement of work done and the sum of money agreed. There is no set format for writing an invoice. However, it should state the date, the name and address of the customer, details of work done, and the price. (Fig. 4.)

J. BROWN – CARPENTER

(address and phone number)

INVOICE No 0000

INVOICE

20th January, 19 . . .

A. Smith, Esq.
(address)

	£
To: Manufacture of one bedside cabinet in pine	400
Delivery	25
	£425

Settlement is requested within 30 days.

Fig. 4   A sample invoice

Every invoice should show an invoice or order number. These are usually applied with a number stamp. The invoices are then filed in order so that any query can be quickly resolved.

Invoices are particularly useful if there is a steady stream of work from a client or customer. It could be inconvenient to meet the customer regularly to ask for money. Instead a weekly or monthly invoice can be sent, asking for the money due for that period.

When the invoice has been paid by the customer a note should be made on your copy of the invoice.

We need say little about the paperwork involved in purchasing goods and materials. The supplier submits an invoice for the money he requires, which you then pay. Once a business is established, regular suppliers will send a monthly statement requesting payment.

Costing and quotes

Costing a job or product is very important. By setting the right price you determine whether or not you cover all your costs and how much you make on top – i.e. *profit*. Costing requires thought. If your business is very small you might prefer to try the market by asking a reasonable figure and adjusting it as your experience grows. In some areas of trade, there might be a standard price for your service or product. You will not be able to deviate from it, but at the same time, judicious enquiry amongst your competition will save you the effort of doing your own costing. Note that in the case of a professional person, the scale of fees to be charged may possibly be outlined by that profession's governing body.

If you are in the position of estimating your own charges, you would generally expect that if you charge less than the competition you may get more business and if you charge too much you will lose business. But paradoxically the reverse is sometimes true! Some people will avoid a product that is "too cheap" because they feel either the product is shoddy or that you are uncertain of your talents. So there are occasions when confidence and a high price will attract custom, simply because your customer thinks that he is getting higher quality. Do not under-price just because you are unsure of yourself.

There are two ways of estimating a satisfactory price for your product, depending on whether you are costing a one-off or a production run.

Costing a one-off job

Examples are the photographer who is asked to quote for,

say, a portrait sitting and the engineer asked to design and manufacture a single component.

When you start in business you want to find out the *unit price* for materials you use regularly. For instance, the photographer who uses film, developing chemicals and photographic paper, will need to establish how much each piece of paper and how much each film costs him. Remember that if you are trading you will buy a considerable quantity of material and may be able to make savings by ordering in bulk. Each unit of material will therefore be cheaper. The unit price is found by dividing the cost of what you have bought by the quantity. For instance, twenty rolls of film bought for £40 gives a unit price of £40 ÷ 20 = £2 per film.

Use the following procedure to find out the price to charge for your product or service:

Materials required: Decide what materials you will need for the job, including wastage.

Unit costs: Find out the unit price of each of these materials and write them down. For example:

Film	£2 per roll
Developing chemicals	50p per roll of film processed
Photographic paper	40p per sheet

Total materials costs: This unit price – the price that each piece or quantity of material costs you – can then be multiplied by the quantity that you expect to use for the job for which you are quoting. In the case of our photographer, he may decide he will need three rolls of film, enough chemicals to develop the film and twenty sheets of paper. By simple multiplication, the photographer can work out how much his materials will cost him:

		£
Film	3 rolls at £2 per roll	6.00
Chemicals	3 rolls of film developed	
	at 50p per roll	1.50
Photographic paper	20 sheets at 40p	8.00
		£15.50

Although we have used the example of a photographer, the principle of finding out the unit price and multiplying it by the quantity used, can be applied to any material used in your particular trade or craft.

Charge for overheads: Add a small charge to cover your general expenses while working on the job. Many small businessmen forget that their general costs must be paid somehow. Such expenses (*overheads* is the technical term) will include rent, heating and lighting, postage, stationery, telephone bills, advertising and miscellaneous. As your only source of income is your sales, spreading these general costs thinly amongst your clients or customers is the only way of budgeting against bills which will roll in whether you are trading or not.

Calculation of the size of this charge for overheads need only be done periodically. Record it as a charge per hour which can be included in your bill to customers. It will not need to be amended until your expenses change dramatically.

How is the hourly charge arrived at?

First, estimate how many hours you can reasonably expect to work in a year. When you start a business you will quickly discover that you may work many more than the traditional forty hours a week. Nevertheless, say that you will work eight hours a day, five days a week for fifty weeks a year. This allows two weeks for holiday. The number of working hours in the year is therefore 40 × 50 or 2,000.

You know what your workshop rent will be. If you have just started trading, you may have to estimate your other expenses, based on personal experience. There is no need to be highly accurate. Indeed this may be impossible at first.

Add together your total estimated overhead expenses and divide by 2,000. This will be the cost of running your business for one hour.

You should be able to anticipate how long any particular job will take. By multiplying the number of hours by the hourly overhead charge you can arrive at a figure to charge your customer.

Performing the calculation is considerably quicker than writing about it, and with practice can be done in a few minutes. A sample calculation is given in Fig. 5.

NAME OF OVERHEAD		ESTIMATED COST FOR YEAR
		£
Rent		3000
Rates		1000
Vehicle expenses		2000
Telephone charges		500
Heating and lighting		1000
Postage, stationery and miscellaneous		500
Total estimated overheads for year		8000
Divide by number of working hours in year, say	÷	2000
		£ 4

If job will take ten hours, total charge to customer is £4 × 10 = £40.

Fig. 5   Calculating a charge for general expenses

Labour charge

There are two sorts of labour charge – that which you charge for your own time, and a charge for the time taken by any employees.

What value you set on your own time and skill depends on your market, your reputation, your training and your field. For instance, a skilled consultant architect's charges will be many times larger than those of a struggling potter or artist who is relatively unknown. The value you place on yourself, your time and skill is something only you can decide.

If your business is larger and you employ a labour force, costing their time is more complex. Allocate a charge out rate to each employee based on his skill and how much you pay him plus overheads. When costing a job, plan ahead as to how many employees will be involved and charge their time according to the charge out rate you have calculated for each of them.

Profit margin

So far we have assessed the level of the price needed to cover material costs, general expenses and time. You should also expect a bonus (over and above the rate you charge for your own time) to justify being in business. This profit margin can be between 5% and 10% of your costs.

Contingencies

Murphy's Law says that if anything can go wrong, it will. Whatever you estimate as the cost of a job, something is bound to be more expensive or take longer than you anticipated. To cover yourself against unexpected delay and expenses, reckon to charge an additional 5 – 10% of your costs in most businesses.

A complete costing for a job is shown in Fig. 6.

When you have completed your estimate for a job to your satisfaction, record the costing in the Order Book. Send a letter to the potential customer (if he or she is not a personal caller) thanking them for their enquiry and offering your quote (see Fig. 2, page 21). Do not give the detailed breakdown of costs given above. The customer would not be interested in the internal mechanics of your business, or, worse, might query certain items!

It is a traditional maxim that the customer is always right. But this is nonsense when it comes to the customer telling

Costing for bedside cabinet

	£	£
Material costs		
Wood	50.00	
Glue, stain and varnish	2.00	
Screws – 2 dozen @ unit price of 20p per dozen	0.40	
	52.40	
Charge for overheads		
20 hours production time @ £4 per hour	80.00	
Labour		
20 hours @ £10 per hour	200.00	
TOTAL COSTS		332.40
Profit margin		
10% of total costs (£332.40)		33.24
Contingency reserve		
10% of total costs (£332.40)		33.24
Price to be charged		£398.88

Say £400.

Fig. 6   A complete costing

you what your price should be! He should trust your integrity. If you are satisfied that your quote is realistic you should not generally be prepared to haggle over the price. Your customer will prefer you to make a sensible estimate and stick to it. If you underprice yourself to obtain a contract and subsequently ask for more money, the customer will have every reason to complain and your reputation will suffer.

Costing a production run

If you run a stall or a shop or a business producing a number of similar products, then you will want to know how to arrive at a realistic price to charge for each item.

The process of costing a production run is not greatly different from that of costing a commission.

The first step is to calculate or estimate your material costs for the whole production run. This estimate can be based on the material costs for each item multiplied by the number of items you intend to produce. Or you can estimate the quantity of material you will need for the entire production run and obtain a quote for a bulk purchase from your suppliers.

Calculate, if you have not already done so, the proportion of your general expenses which the business incurs each hour, as explained on page 26.

Calculate the labour charge for the production run by multiplying your hourly labour charge, plus that for any staff you may employ, by the number of hours you expect to take to produce a set number of items.

Take about 10% of the total of material, overhead and labour charge and allow this twice, once for a profit margin and again for a "buffer" against unexpected contingencies.

The grand total of all these expected costs can now be divided by the number of items you expect to produce (so long as you are sure of selling them all). This will give the price you should charge per item. (Fig. 7.)

Officialdom and book-keeping

When you run your own business you take responsibility for your own financial affairs so, you need to understand the steps the government expects you to take.

The Inland Revenue

The government agency responsible for collecting Income Tax in the United Kingdom is the Inland Revenue.

As a self-employed person you are expected to account for your income. Every year on 5th April you will receive a form

Costing one hundred bookends

	£	£
Material costs		
Wood – bought in bulk	90.00	
Glue, stain and varnish	2.00	
Screws – 600 (or 50 dozen) @ unit price of 20p per dozen	10.00	
	102.00	
Charge for overheads		
Anticipated half an hour per item = 50 hours production time @ £4	200.00	
Labour		
50 hours at £10 per hour	500.00	
TOTAL COSTS		802.00
Profit margin		
10% of total costs (£802.00)		80.20
Contingency reserve		
10% of total costs (£802.00)		80.20
Price to be charged for one hundred items		£962.40

Price per bookend: $\dfrac{962.40}{100}$ = £9.62

Fig. 7   Costing each item in a production run

called a Tax Return on which you must enter all income received during the year.

If you are considering self-employment, you should write to your nearest Inland Revenue office and inform them of your intentions. The address will be in the telephone book. Even if you are only trading part-time, you should still tell the Tax Inspector what you are doing. He will probably do nothing at this stage but he will be aware of your plans and forward the relevant forms at the proper time.

It is sometimes worth making personal contact with the person who will handle your tax affairs. This has a double advantage. You may see bureaucracy in a kinder light and your face will mean more to the tax officer than a number on a file.

National Insurance contributions

Most people working in the United Kingdom have to pay National Insurance contributions.

When you are employed by a firm they are deducted automatically by the employer and paid directly to the Department of Social Security (DSS). The self-employed, however, must make their contributions directly.

There are various classes of contributions you can make. Class 2 entitles you to all benefits except unemployment benefit. Class 4 is related to profits. All self-employed people should consider making contributions to a private pension scheme.

Consult your nearest DSS office for advice in your personal case.

Value Added Tax

In the United Kingdom and Isle of Man, a direct tax is levied on most business transactions. This is Value Added Tax, or VAT, and is covered in greater detail in Chapter 6, page 85.

If you anticipate a substantial turnover in your business, in excess of the VAT threshold (which may vary from year to year – enquire at the VAT office), then you must register with the Customs and Excise VAT department.

There are two other matters which should be settled before you start trading – the question of a bank account for the business and making provision for life insurance and a pension.

A bank account

It is helpful to open a separate bank account for all business transactions. This certainly applies if your business is of any size, but should be considered even if your enterprise is small. By keeping a separate account you are in a better position to judge the state of your business finances, as they are then distinct from your personal affairs.

It is worth pointing out that most clearing banks will allow you to open what is called a second, or No. 2 personal account, which may then be used exclusively for business purposes. If you open a formal business account you may pay higher charges!

Pension schemes and insurances

If you pay Class 2 National Insurance contributions, you will be entitled to a State pension. By contributing to a private pension scheme or having an insurance policy, you may be able to make provision for more substantial remuneration on retirement. Consult a specialist adviser such as an insurance broker or accountant on this complex subject.

As a self-employed person you will have no source of income if you are sick, injured or otherwise prevented from earning a living. Unless you have plenty of money, take out adequate insurance against such an eventuality. You may begrudge the payment of the premiums but you really have no alternative!

Sources of finance

You may be eligible for a government grant or loan towards establishing your business. Enquiries should be made at the nearest office of the Department of Trade.

4

Counting the cost

From the first day of trading, careful track must be kept of everything spent, and all money received. It is easy to think that early payments do not matter because they are small, but even these add up, and it is vital to get into the habit of recording income and expenditure. Never delay recording transactions for more than a month. Otherwise the result can be confusion and errors. Discipline is essential in keeping an accurate cash book.

The cash book

The most important record to keep is a *cash book*. This will form a summary of the money you receive and the money you spend. It need not actually be a book at all. A number of loose sheets in a file or binder, or a child's exercise book will do. However, purpose-made books can be purchased for a very reasonable sum from office suppliers. These are generally well-made with good quality paper and are printed with the columns needed to make entries.

If you wish to produce your own cash sheets, this can be done as follows:

Take a piece of A4 or foolscap paper and lay it before you. With a pencil or pen rule a number of parallel lines right across the page starting at the top and working down. The gap between the lines should be $3/8''$ or 1 cm. Then divide the page into a number of columns, about $1''$ (2.5 cm) wide. (Fig. 8.)

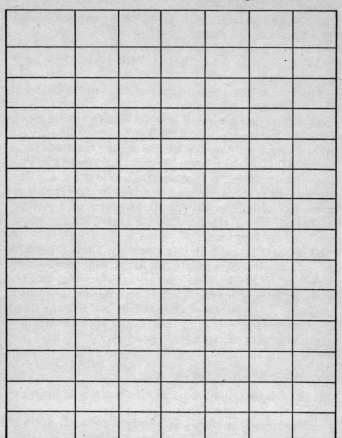

Fig. 8   Drawing up a master cash sheet

This page forms the master copy for your cash book sheets and can be photocopied (at a copy shop or library) to give you sufficient sheets for a year's records, which can be kept in a loose-leaf or ring file. All that is required is two pages for each month's trading, one to record the money received and the other to record money spent.

The most important rule in book-keeping is: KEEP ALL INVOICES AND BILLS THAT YOU PAY. These serve two purposes.

Firstly, it is from them that you will record the entries in the cash book.

Secondly, they are proof that the item concerned was a genuine business expense. If the Tax Inspector should ever want to check up, you must be able to show him the invoice as proof that you have spent the money. So make sure that your name and the date appear on the receipt or bill, and that receipts are properly stamped or signed by the supplier. A mere note of the amount you spent, written on a piece of notepaper, is unlikely to satisfy the taxman except where amounts are very small.

Once the bill is paid, file it immediately. The best way is to use a concertina, lever arch or ring file. A cardboard box will serve at a pinch. You can either file the receipts alphabetically, using the name of the supplier, or in date order, placing each receipt on top of the last. For very small businesses, date order filing is adequate. The point is that it must be easy to extract any desired item.

Recording movements of money

Money will, hopefully, flow into the business as items are sold.

Unfortunately it often seems to flow right out again as various expenses arise. So, this is our first distinction – between money in *(receipts)* and money out *(payments)*.

Note that the word receipt can have two meanings. People often think of a receipt as an acknowledgement of payment they receive from a trader; viz. "Can I have a receipt for the purchase, please?"

In book-keeping the term receipt is more usually applied to "money in", or the money received for sales or other services.

Open the cash book to the first double page. If you have prepared your own cash sheets open the file so that you have two sheets in front of you side by side.

It is customary to record "money in", i.e. receipts, on the left hand page, although there is no need to follow this convention. It is convenient only because it is easier to remember – money comes IN on the left and flows OUT on the right.

You will notice that the cash book has a number of vertical columns marked up for entering sums of money: pounds and pence, or the currency of the country in which you live.

Take a pencil and head up the left hand page "receipts" and the right hand page "payments".

Where does money come from?

Look at the "money in" side of the cash book – the left hand page. Think about the various kinds of money you will receive.

The most obvious source of money will be *sales*, that is, money you actually receive from selling your wares or services.

So, on the left hand page, count six columns in from the left and write SALES above the column.

From time to time you may expect odd receipts, money from unexpected sources. You might sell your car, for instance, or receive an insurance claim. It is as well to have a column marked OTHER INCOME or SUNDRY INCOME. Write this at the top of the next column along.

The left hand page of your cash book should now appear as Fig. 9.

Now let us deal with the five blank columns on the left. The first one is easy. You want to know when you received the money, so head this column DATE.

For record purposes it is useful to know the person or firm from which the money came. So, write SOURCE, or DESCRIPTION, above the next TWO columns. The spaces in these columns can also be used for making a brief note

			RECEIPTS PAGE			
					SALES	OTHER INCOME

Fig. 9   Receipts page heading

about a receipt.

We now have ways of identifying almost everything about each sum of money received; there is only one other thing we do not know and this can be very useful. After you received the money did you keep it in your pocket as cash or did you, as is more common with cheques you may receive, pay it into your bank? This we can show in the two remaining columns on the receipts page. Write BANKED over the first, and CASH RETAINED over the second.

If all has gone well, the left hand page of your book should now be headed as in Fig. 10.

			RECEIPTS PAGE			
DATE	SOURCE OR DESCRIPTION OF INCOME	BANKED	CASH RETAINED	SALES	OTHER INCOME	

Fig. 10   Receipts page heading completed

You have now set up the receipts, or money in, side of your cash book. Turn the pages of the cash book and repeat the headings on the next few left hand pages. If you have just started trading, and the number of receipts is low, then you probably only need one page a month. If this is the case, start by heading up twelve pages. You can always add more if you need to.

You can now fill in all the details of money you received in the first day or week. The two places you will find these details are in the paying-in book and in your invoice book. You should have been making a note in the invoice book every time someone paid you. If you have been paid, check to see that you have the money to hand. Record the total you are paying into the bank in the paying-in book and keep a note of the sum you are retaining as cash.

Now enter these figures in the cash book:

Open the cash book on the first left hand page. Look at the copy of the invoice and note the date you received the money and from whom. Write these details on the first line of the *receipts* page. Was the sum banked? If it was, write the amount under *banked*. If it was cash and stayed in your pocket, then write the amount under *cash retained*.

All right so far?

Now decide what the money was for. If it was for a sale, or a job you did, then enter the amount again under sales.

Let us take the case of the carpenter we met in Chapter 2, who is recording the sale of the bedside cabinet for which he quoted. The entry would be made as in Fig 11.

People often wonder why the sum of money is entered twice when it is received only once. The point is that we are recording two pieces of information: firstly, where the money came from (that is, sales), and, secondly, what was done with the money, i.e. whether it was banked or stayed in the pocket as ready cash.

Then go onto the next invoice and repeat the process, writing the details onto the next line of the cash book.

When all the sales have been recorded, have another

		RECEIPTS PAGE			
DATE	SOURCE OR DESCRIPTION OF INCOME	BANKED	CASH RETAINED	SALES	OTHER INCOME
5th FEBRUARY	Mr SMITH - SALE OF BEDSIDE CABINET	425.00		425.00	

Fig. 11 Recording a sale

glance through the records. Were there any receipts which were not sales?

If there were, record them in the same way. First the date, and then the source of the money. Was something else sold – a tool perhaps? Perhaps a gift was received? Write the amount under the column entitled *other* income.

Two examples are given in Fig. 12.

		RECEIPTS PAGE			
DATE	SOURCE OR DESCRIPTION OF INCOME	BANKED	CASH RETAINED	SALES	OTHER INCOME
5th FEBRUARY	Mr SMITH - SALE OF BEDSIDE CABINET	425.00		425.00	
7th FEBRUARY	SALE OF DRILL		25.00		25.00
9th FEBRUARY	Mr JONES GIFT		5.00		5.00

Fig. 12 Recording sundry income

Loans can be a complication in a set of accounts, but the procedure for recording the receipt of the money is the same as the items we have mentioned above. Again, note the date you received the loan, the source, e.g. the name of the bank, and enter the amount of money received in both columns. A substantial loan would be probably paid into the bank straight away. So enter the figure once in the *banked* column, and again under the *other income* column.

All the receipts for the day or week should be entered. Check once more to make sure that none have been forgotten or overlooked.

If the type of business involves the sale of a few expensive items then each sale should be recorded separately. If, however, you run a stall or are engaged in some other venture which involves the sale of a number of small items, then clearly it would be ridiculous to record every single sale in the cash book. At the end of each day or week a lump sum will be banked. When entering up the cash book in this case it is necessary only to record the date that the money was paid in, and the fact that the sum derived from sales. Again enter the sum twice; under sales, and under the cash banked column (or the cash column if the cash is retained for everyday use).

If you do not actually sell anything, but make a living by offering a service, for instance, a chimney sweep, or a landscape gardener, then the procedure will be just the same. Instead of the sales column in your cash book you will have a column entitled FEES RECEIVED. Otherwise the cash book is completed in the same way.

Repeat this process every day, or week, as time allows.

The monthly summary

At the end of each month it is best to rule off each page and start the new month on a fresh page. This gives you the opportunity to total all the various receipts in the month and check that the month's records are complete.

Glance down the page to confirm that you have entered

each amount twice. Now with a calculator, or manually, add the entries in each column. Record the total of each column at the bottom of the page. You will then be able to see at a glance how much cash was received in the month, and whether it was paid into the bank or kept in the hand.

Did you miss anything out? The one sure way to check is to take your sales and sundry income totals and add them up. They should equal the combined total of the banked and cash retained columns (Fig. 13). This technique is called *cross-casting*.

If the totals do not balance then you have omitted to enter a figure twice, or you have added the vertical columns wrongly. Re-check and get it right!

You have now mastered the task of keeping track of money coming into the business. Repeat the process for every month of trading and see at a glance what money has come into the business month by month.

Where does it go?

The basic procedure for recording and analysing payments is identical to that for receipts. The main difference is the number of columns across the page. The reason for this is that there were only two types of income: sales and sundry income. The various types of expenditure are usually more numerous.

Look through the file of bills that have been paid during the day or week, select one at random and study it. Like the bills you sent out to other people (Fig. 4, page 23) it will include the name of the supplier, the date, a description of the purchases and how much was spent. There will be one other item that will not at this stage have been entered on the invoices: that is any tax, such as (in the U.K.) VAT (Value Added Tax). This need not worry us at this stage if the business is not subject to VAT registration. Such registration is only necessary or advisable if you anticipate a substantial *turnover* in the first months or year of trading. Turnover is simply your gross sales in a given period. If you

DATE	SOURCE OR DESCRIPTION OF INCOME		BANKED	CASH RETAINED	SALES	OTHER INCOME
		RECEIPTS PAGE				
5th FEBRUARY	Mr SMITH - SALE OF BEDSIDE CABINET		425.00		425.00	
7th FEBRUARY	SALE OF DRILL			25.00		25.00
9th FEBRUARY	Mr JONES GIFT			5.00		5.00
15th FEBRUARY	SALES		325.19		325.19	
20th FEBRUARY	SALE OF EGG CUPS			15.85	15.85	
25th FEBRUARY	SALES		105.35		105.35	
28th FEBRUARY	SALE OF CHEST OF DRAWERS		209.10		209.10	
TOTAL			1064.64	45.85	1080.49	30.00

Check for Accuracy: 1064.64 + 45.85   1080.49 + 30.00

= 1110.49   = 1110·49

Fig. 13   Summarising the month's receipts

think you may be in this position turn now to Chapter 6, page 90, for advice on procedure. VAT registration will affect the construction of the cash book.

AMOS &Co
TIMBER MERCHANTS
Address and VAT No.

2 February 19XX

TO: Mr BROWN

INVOICE No. 0000

GOODS		
20m. 10cm. sq. Pine	50	—
VAT at 15%	7	50
TOTAL £	57	50

Fig. 14   A sample invoice for payment

But if you do not anticipate earning a great deal at first, then ignore the tax figure on the bills received. You will pay the total at the bottom of the invoice, which includes VAT, and it is this figure that you will record in the cash book.

A sample bill is shown in Fig. 14. You want to record all these details in the cash book.

Open the cash book again but this time use the right hand (payments) page. Just as with the receipts page you have a number of columns. The exact number will depend on the different types of expenditure that will be incurred.

The first thing you need to know about the payment is when it was made. Take a pencil and entitle the first column *date*. This will not be the date on the bill but the date it was paid, which may or may not be the same thing.

The next thing to record is the name of the supplier and to note a brief description of the goods, so at the top of the next two columns write *supplier or description*.

As a number of payments will be by cheque, it is useful to have some cross-reference to the cheque book. As each cheque is written, record the last three digits of the cheque number in the cash book in the next column along, which you will entitle *cheque number*.

Receipts were either banked or retained as petty cash for everyday expenses. Similarly, when bills are paid it will be either by cheque or cash. Again you want to distinguish between the two, so your next two column headings are: BANK PAYMENT and CASH PAYMENT. (Fig. 15).

Providing the cash book or sheets are wide enough there should still be room for at least ten columns. Into them will go all the various categories of expenditure which are connected with the business.

What these are will vary considerably according to the type of business. Some will apply only to one trade, for example, picture framing for an artist. Others, like postage and telephone, will apply to almost everyone. Think about all the various types of expenditure you have, or anticipate encountering in the course of running the business and make a list on a separate piece of paper.

DATE	SUPPLIER OR DESCRIPTION	CHQ No.	BANK PAYMENT	CASH PAYMENT	

Fig. 15 Bank and cash payments headings

Artist	*Writer*	*Labourer*	*Engineer*	*Potter*
Paint	Travel	Tools	Materials	Clay
Canvas	Paper	Travel	Tooling	Glazes
Brushes	Postage	Protective	costs	Advertising
Exhibition		Clothing	Wages	Loose
Costs				Equipment
Framing and				Exhibition
Reprographic				Costs
Expenses				

Fig. 16 A selection of specific costs in various trades

Fig. 16 gives a small selection of the sorts of expenditure met with in different trades. If your business is not included, construct your own list.

Types of expenditure common to almost every type of business are as follows:

Materials
Stationery
Postage
Telephone
Travel & subsistence
Car expenses

Rent and rates
Heat and lighting
Wages and labour costs
Miscellaneous expenses
Advertising

Note that expenses for travelling to and from your home and principal place of work cannot be claimed against tax.

Enter in the cash book all expenses connected with the business. All expenses entered in the cash book must be genuine and where possible supported by the bills which were paid. The Tax Inspector has the right to inspect your records if he suspects expenses are being claimed which have not really been incurred. At the same time do not hesitate to include bona fide expenses if they may be allowable against tax.

There are two things to notice before we start entitling the columns in the cash book.

First, if you are working from home, then some items (for example telephone bills) will consist partly of expenditure on business use, and partly private use. The same may apply to a private vehicle and its running costs if it is used partly for business. It can be very difficult to split these bills accurately. At this stage it is best to enter the full amount of bills paid in the cash book. An estimated percentage for private use can always be extracted when you come to draw up final accounts. If you do not intend to draw up your own accounts but instead submit your cash book either to the Tax Inspector (not recommended) or an accountant then you could leave the job of making this estimate to them.

The second point is that you can group different expenditure under a single heading. For instance there is no need to distinguish between materials used in the manufacture of goods. There is no point, for example, in a photographer having separate columns for film, developing paper, chemicals and so on. These are all materials used in the production of photographs and can be listed as such.

Similarly, if you find yourself running short of columns in the cash book, related types of expenditure can be listed together – for example rent and rates; or postage and stationery. You can always re-analyse these columns later if so desired.

The remaining columns in the cash book can now be given their headings. Work from left to right across the page.

Direct costs

Start with costs DIRECTLY involved in the cost of the product. In the case of most manufacturing industries this means starting with MATERIALS. There is an important distinction between costs which are built into the product, and the general expenses arising from being in business. To illustrate this take the example of the carpenter we met in Chapter 2. The direct costs of producing a bedside cabinet will be the wood, glue, screws and other materials which make up the product.

General overheads

Telephone charges, loose tools, casual labour, and so on are general expenses, or OVERHEADS, incurred by the carpenter in the course of business, regardless of whether he produces the bedside cabinet.

So head up the columns in the cash book, starting with the direct costs involved in the product, and then entering the various types of general overheads.

Try to leave two columns blank at the right of the page. You will see why in a moment.

If all has gone right, the page should look like Fig. 17. The example given is that of an artist's cash book.

Why have we left two columns? There are two other types of expenditure which still need to be explained. They will be treated differently when drawing up final accounts and should therefore be shown separately in the cash book.

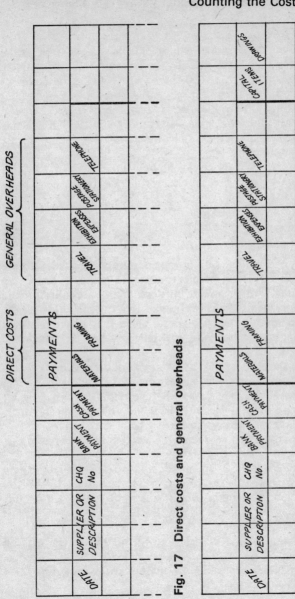

Fig. 17 Direct costs and general overheads

Fig. 18 The payments page complete

Fixed assets

If you buy or introduce equipment which is essential for the business, and which will last for some time, it is a relatively permanent asset of the business and is called a *fixed asset* or *capital item*. There are generally three types of capital expenditure: *motor vehicles, plant and equipment* and *furniture and fittings*. In short any expensive item which is an integral part of the business, is essential to it, and will last a long time.

Head up the first blank column *capital items*. Under this heading we will enter any item which falls into one of these categories.

Personal expenses

There is one final sort of expenditure associated with the business. This is payment made to yourself for living expenses or other private purposes. These are called private withdrawals or *drawings* for short. Write this title over the last column on the page. Enter under it all expenses which are not connected with the business but for which the business has paid.

The skeleton for the payments side of the cash book is now complete. You can if you like transfer the headings to each of the next twelve pages. As with the receipts it is best if one, or two, pages are allocated to each month's payments. A new month should always be started on a fresh page.

The completed payments page will now appear as in Fig. 18.

How often the payments side of the cash book is written up will depend on the amount of business done. If there are many entries to make it may be easier to enter them in one session every month. Otherwise a few minutes every day or week should suffice.

Some may find it easiest to record the details of each payment in the cash book every time they write a cheque. Cash payments can then be entered at the same time.

PAYMENTS

DATE	SUPPLIER OR DESCRIPTION	CHQ No	BANK PAYMENT	CASH PAYMENT	MATERIALS	FRAMING	TRAVEL	EXHIBITIONS EXPENSES	POSTAGE STATIONERY	TELEPHONE	CAPITAL ITEMS	DRAWINGS
2 FEB	TIMMS & Co GOODS	756	100.00		100.00							
4 FEB	CASH	757	20.00									20.00
5 FEB	PETROL			5.00			5.00					

Fig. 19   Sample payments

When entering payments, have beside you the cheque book and the pile of bills which have accumulated over the period. One by one record the details of each bill, checking it off against the cheque book and recording the date on which it was paid. If it is known that a bill was paid and there is no record in the cheque book, then it must have been a cash transaction. Enter the full amount in the cash payment column.

Then, on the same line, enter the amount again under the relevant heading: e.g. materials, private, travel, etc. It will be noted that again the amount is entered twice, the first time to show how it was paid, i.e. by cheque or with cash; the second time to reveal what type of expenditure it was. (Fig. 19).

Continue the process for all payments made in the period. Do not forget to include under drawings any cheques written for private spending money or other personal expenses. There is no need to keep careful track of *cash* spent on personal expenses (except from the view of the domestic budget!). This would complicate the records. A record of the cheques drawn from the business for such private expenditure is all that is required. The word *cash* should be written in the *description* column.

The monthly summary

At the end of the month, rule off the page across the bottom. Add up the amount in each column and record that total at the bottom of the page.

Once again, check whether everything has been entered, and that the columns have been added up correctly. This is done, as with the receipts, by adding the individual totals along the bottom of the page and checking to see whether they equal the sum of the bank payment and cash payment columns. See Fig. 20.

If the totals agree, then you have mastered the technique for keeping a cash book. Kept properly, these few sheets will reveal all that you need to know about the movements of cash into and out of the business. If you found it difficult,

DATE	SUPPLIER OR DESCRIPTION	CHQ No.	BANK PAYMENT	CASH PAYMENT	MATERIALS	FRAMING	TRAVEL	EXHIBITION EXPENSES	POSTAGE & STATIONERY	TELEPHONE	CAPITAL ITEMS	DRAWINGS
					PAYMENTS							
2 FEB	TIMMS & Co GOODS	756	100.00		100.00							
4 FEB	CASH	757	20.00									20.00
5 FEB	PETROL			5.00			5.00					
15 FEB	PETROL	758	15.00				15.00					
25 FEB	CASH DRAWINGS	759	250.00									250.00
26 FEB	AMOS & Co	760	10.00			10.00						
28 FEB	Mr JAMES STALL RENT			30.00				30.00				
TOTAL			395.00	35.00	100.00	10.00	20.00	30.00				270.00

Check for Accuracy: 395.00 + 35.00 = 430

100.00 + 10.00 + 20.00 + 30.00 + 270.00 = 430

Fig. 20 Summarising the month's payments

rest assured the task will be very much easier the next time.

Problems

Most expenses which you encounter will be straightforward and easy to record. There are however three categories of expenditure which may cause confusion:

How to record loan repayments and hire purchase payments;

The distinction between wages, casual labour and sub-contract;

Bank charges and standing orders.

Recording repayments of loans and hire purchase

These are complicated by the fact that there is not only a repayment of capital but also the interest which accumulates during the term of the agreement. At the stage of completing the cash book entries, we are only recording the actual flow of cash into and out of the business. The task is therefore simplified. Do not worry about interest or capital until the accounts are prepared at the end of the financial year.

All that is recorded in the cash book is the sum which is paid to the bank or the finance house every month. Do not record the full purchase price figure in the cash book. If purchase was made with a loan, or under the terms of a hire purchase agreement the business has not actually parted with that much cash. The only figures which belong in the cash book are the monthly repayments which you make. Merely make sure that you have full details of the agreement so that you may consult them when drawing up the year-end accounts. If you do not intend to prepare your own accounts, then the accountant or Tax Inspector will wish to see them.

Wages, casual labour and sub-contract.

The distinction between these is important.

Wages are payments made to workers who are employed on a regular basis, obeying orders and usually using the company's facilities to assist the proprietor to make a product or provide a service. In the U.K. the employer is responsible for deducting the workers' tax and National Insurance contributions, for adding back any Statutory Sick Pay and submitting the relevant sum to the appropriate authorities. So far as the cash book is concerned the book-keeping requirements are not complicated. Once again, we are at this stage only involved with preparing a record of the movements of cash. Thus the net payments to workers and the regular submission of taxes collected to the Inland Revenue are recorded in the same way as any other payment.

However, the computation of tax, and keeping an accurate record of deductions, can be considerably more time-consuming. The Inland Revenue or an accountant should be consulted before embarking on the employment of a labour force.

There are alternatives which are worth considering, especially if the business is in its infancy.

One such is the employment of *casual labour*. If part-time assistance (below the PAYE and N.I. thresholds) is required, then the employment of someone on a casual basis is probably the best option. If you insist that the assistant is himself self-employed then it may be possible to make lump-sum payments to him (or her) at an agreed rate and leave him to resolve his own tax affairs. It is essential, however, to inform the Tax Inspector in order to avoid any later complications. Once again, because the payment to the worker is by cash or cheque then it should be recorded in the cash book.

A related situation arises in the case of *sub-contract*. The distinction between a sub-contractor and casual labourer is that the sub-contractor is generally an autonomous individual or firm, often with his or her own premises and tools, who will undertake a specific stage in the manufacture of a product or the provision of a service. If for instance you are a publisher, then you could employ skilled editors on a sub-contract basis to do various specialised jobs.

Payments to sub-contractors are usually recorded in a separate column in the cash book. As their charges are often a direct cost of production, record them next to materials.

Bank charges and standing orders.

If bank charges or interest are paid, or you have arranged to pay regular bills by standing or bankers orders, remember that the bank statement will be the only evidence for these payments. It is easy to overlook these when completing the cash book, so, before you rule off each page and summarise the entries for the month, glance through any bank statements you have received in the period. If you have paid any standing orders or bank charges record them in the cash book, once under the heading bank payments, and again under the heading for which the payment was made. In the case of bank charges and interest it is worth heading up a separate column if you anticipate paying these regularly. Otherwise write them into sundry or miscellaneous expenses, making a short note beside them as you do so.

Interpreting the cash book

Much can be learnt from the cash book. The pages are a record of how much is spent each month. They therefore give a picture of the fluctuations in the business's financial affairs which can be used to plan ahead and to remedy mistakes made in the past.

Many owners of small businesses regard the keeping of financial records as a chore. The cash book is regarded as a passive statement of their expenditure, to be filed away until the time comes to draw up the final accounts.

To take this attitude is to court disaster. You cannot run a company, even on a small scale, if the only guides to the financial state of the business are bank statements and intuition.

Many small businesses are forced into bankruptcy every year. In some cases this is the result of genuine misfortune, shrinking markets or rising costs. Frequently, however, the cause is pure lack of financial control. Proprietors fail to monitor progress properly. If the business is doing well, the owner may fail to capitalise on that success and miss useful opportunities for expansion. If there are grounds for concern, he may miss the warning signs until too late. Intelligent use of the cash book can help you to avoid these pitfalls.

The first month or so of trading will probably be unrepresentative. After a period of at least three months you can start to use the cash book as a reasonably accurate guide.

Checking costings

One way to use the cash book is to check the accuracy of costings. If you manufacture products, then your costings will have been based on an estimate of material costs, a proportion of general business overheads, a charge for labour, a profit margin, and an allowance for unforeseen expenses. By comparing the relative levels of sales and material costs and general expenses you can test whether the prices charged are right. If costs are only just covered then you must consider whether customers would tolerate a realistic price increase, and how much that should be.

Perhaps you are in the fortunate position of having a substantial profit margin. That is, sales are considerably more than total expenses. In this case you could consider dropping your prices to attract more custom, and expand. Or you can estimate how much more can be drawn from the business for personal use.

Monitoring costs

Another opportunity created by the cash book is the chance to monitor costs. For instance, on a day-to-day basis, you may not know how much you have spent on materials. By studying the cash book you might see a way to control the level of expenditure if it seems unduly high. By examining the names of suppliers you can, if you require, assess who is your key supplier. Corresponding information about customers may be gleaned from the receipts pages.

Budgeting

Budgeting for the present can be achieved with some accuracy. Let us suppose a van is needed to extend the distribution network. Perhaps you require some necessary but expensive tool. Whether you can afford it will be revealed by the cash book. Work out by simple subtraction how much you have to spare after a month's trading. If there is an excess then you can realistically assess the practicality of buying the new vehicle or equipment. (Fig. 21).

Income in month		1200
Less: Material costs	700	
General overheads	200	
		900
Margin to spare		£300

Fig. 21   Budgeting, using the cash book

Management accounts

You can use the financial picture given in the cash book to project the future of the business. This can be very useful if you need to approach the bank manager for a loan or overdraft. It can also be useful to you as the proprietor. The process needs a little extra arithmetic, but is perfectly straightforward.

After several months trading you will have a good idea of the general levels of expenditure and income to expect each month. Add the monthly totals in each column in the cash book to reach a total for the whole period you have been trading and rewrite them in a vertical format. (Fig. 22).

	DECEMBER £	JANUARY £	FEBRUARY £	TOTAL £
Income				
Sales or fees	1600	1800	1520	4920
Less: Expenditure				
Materials	200	400	400	1000
Postage	50	100	100	250
Telephone	100	100	50	250
Travel	50	20	10	80
Profit (or loss)	1200	1180	960	3340
Add: Other income	—	—	200	200
Less: Drawings	(150)	(100)	(250)	(500)
Cash flow	£1050	£1080	£910	£3040

Fig. 22   Calculating cash flow

Expenditure, including capital items, is subtracted from sales, or fees, received. This will give a profit (or loss) figure. Losses may be indicated by using brackets. To the profit is added other income and the total in the drawings column is then subtracted.

The resulting figure is the cash flow for the period. Divide these totals by the number of months to derive an average for each type of income or expenditure. (Fig. 23.)

This will take care of any monthly fluctuations. The figure you have in each case is the average monthly level. If each averaged figure is multiplied by twelve, we will have an estimate of the cash flow at the end of a year's trading (Fig. 24).

We must assume of course that no major changes occur in the year. Bearing this assumption in mind, it is possible to forecast what the business will achieve in a year.

By performing these simple calculations the businessman can see roughly what he can expect in the way of sales, where

	TOTAL FOR (December + January + March)	DIVIDE BY = 3	MONTHLY AVERAGE
	£		£
Income			
Sales or fees	4920		1640
Expenditure			
Materials	1000		334
Postage	250		83
Telephone	250		83
Travel	80		27
Profit (or loss)	3340		1113
Add: Other income	200		66
Less: Drawings	(500)		(166)
Cash flow	3040		1013

Fig. 23   Calculating monthly average

	MONTHLY AVERAGE	MULTIPLY BY 12	FORECAST FOR YEAR
	£		£
Income			
Sales or fees	1640		19680
Expenditure			
Materials	334		4008
Postage	83		996
Telephone	83		996
Travel	27		324
Profit (or loss)	1113		13356
Add: Other income	66		792
Less: Drawings	(166)		(1992)
Cash flow	1013		12156

Fig. 24   Forecasting yearly cash flow

he might reduce expenditure, and where he might increase his income in order to achieve a healthy year-end picture.

Should the bank manager or other party want to examine the prospects of a business, such a projected forecast will aid him in his task.

5

Called to account

After a business has been trading for some months or a year, the financial records which are contained in the cash book are summarised to produce an account.

Accounting dates

The most important date in the U.K.'s financial calendar is 5th April. This day marks the end of the tax year and it is then, not 31st December, that tax return forms are issued, wages records summarised and some (but by no means all) company accounts are finalised.

The reason for this curious date being chosen is worth a digression.

For many hundreds of years the calendar was based on the old Julian calendar, which was developed in Roman times. By 1752 scholars had noted that the actual dates in the calendar had begun to lag behind changes in the natural seasons. So it was that in that year Pope Gregory decreed that eleven days should be struck from the calendar. Many people were concerned at this apparent loss of several days but none more so than the Inland Revenue.

Under the old calendar, the financial year ended with the winter quarter in March, and 25th March, or Lady Day, marked the beginning of the new year.

Worried lest they be asked to forfeit eleven days revenue the tax authorities accepted the new Gregorian calendar but altered their new year's day by eleven days to 5th April.

There is no need to finalise your accounts on 5th April. Any convenient date may be chosen. Many businessmen pick a point one year after they start trading, which may be 31st May, 16th September or indeed any day. The tax authorities will allocate profits between one tax year and the next, and the proportion which applies after 5th April will be treated as belonging in the next financial year. The calculation (or *tax computation*) which this involves requires much specialised knowledge and is something which an amateur cannot really tackle.

There are, however, certain guidelines for choosing a date on which to end the financial year.

If you were to pick 31st March or 5th April then you would receive the maximum benefit of any allowance you might be due. To receive these in full, is, of course, a good thing. The drawback of using dates close to the end of the official tax year is that if you have made profits which are taxable, then you will be required to pay any tax due immediately.

Consider, therefore, ending the accounting year on a date shortly after 5th April, such as 30th April. In this way, under British tax law, you will receive most of the allowances to which you are entitled. However, any tax payable on profits will not be due for another year, which can be a help if at first money is tight.

Tax law is an extremely complex subject and it may be worth consulting an accountant or tax specialist before deciding on which date to finalise records. In general terms, 30th April is a good choice.

The first year

It is unnecessary to prepare accounts after less than six month's trading. For instance, if you chose 30th April as year-end, and you only started trading in January, the Tax Inspector should not expect a complete set of accounts for the trading you have accomplished in only four months.

The more usual procedure in the first year of trading is to tack the initial few months onto the next full year. Thus, if a business was started in January of one year the accounts are prepared sixteen months later, that is, on 30th April of the next. (Fig. 25).

Fig. 25   Choosing an accounting date – business commences in January

If on the other hand trading was started half way through the financial year, then accounts would be made up for the six months between that date and 30th April. (Fig. 26).

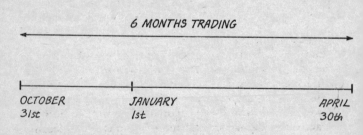

Fig. 26   Choosing an accounts date – business starts in middle of tax year

After your initial trading period your tax affairs will be consistent and you can prepare accounts at the end of each full year. (Fig. 27).

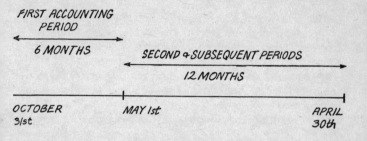

Fig. 27   Second and subsequent accounting years

Once you have chosen a date on which to end each period of trading it is best to stick to it in subsequent years.

Submitting accounts

As stated on page 10, the tax authorities *will* accept financial records without a summary or a set of formal accounts. You may, if you so wish, deliver to them bills for everything purchased. Together with a note of sales, this will be sufficient to assess tax liability.

While this approach to book-keeping is acceptable it carries the disadvantage that it is difficult to monitor the health of the business on a day-to-day basis, or to check the Tax Inspector's calculations.

If you decide to use an accountant for preparation of final accounts, the neater and more complete the records then the less the accountant needs to do, and consequently the smaller his bill.

Maintaining a proper cash book is not difficult. Summarising it and producing a small set of accounts is no more complicated.

Summarising the cash book

After you have decided upon a date to end your financial year, you need do no more than make your regular entries in the cash book until after that date has passed. After that the cash book can be summarised. This means that the individual totals from each month are entered on a separate page of the cash book and added to give a complete picture of the year's (or period's) trading.

The summary can, if you wish, be drawn up on a separate

MONTH	BANKED	CASH RETAINED	SALES	OTHER INCOME			
MAY							
JUNE							
JULY							
AUGUST							
SEPTEMBER							
OCTOBER							
NOVEMBER							
DECEMBER							
JANUARY							
FEBRUARY							
MARCH							
APRIL							
YEARLY TOTALS							

Fig. 28   Annual summary – receipts

MONTHS	BANK PAYMENTS	CASH PAYMENTS	MATERIALS	OTHER EXPENSE HEADINGS							
MAY											
JUNE											
JULY											
AUGUST											
SEPTEMBER											
OCTOBER											
NOVEMBER											
DECEMBER											
JANUARY											
FEBRUARY											
MARCH											
APRIL											
YEARLY TOTALS											

Fig. 29 Annual summary – payments

piece of paper, but it is neatest to complete the summary in the cash book itself. Any transactions made while writing up the summary would be entered in the next year's record on the next page on.

When the cash book was filled in, the entries should have been summarised at the end of each month. If this has not been done, now is the time. See pages 52 to 54.

Then turn to the two pages you have selected for your summary and write in column headings, just as you have before, checking back to make sure you do not miss one.

Down the left hand margin of each page write in the months of the year or period in which you have been trading. For instance if trading was begun in May and you are summarising your records at the 30th April the summary will appear as in Figs. 28 and 29.

The appropriate totals may now be entered alongside each date.

Turn to the pages recording the first month of trading and transfer each total from the bottom of the page to the appropriate line in the summary. For instance, if in May the total cash banked was £1,000, transfer this figure to the summary, entering it in the cash banked column opposite May. Work horizontally across the page, transferring each total from the monthly page to the summary until all the totals for that month are accounted for. (Figs. 30 and 31).

Check to see that you have not missed one.

This process may then be repeated for every other month in the cash book until all monthly totals appear on the summary.

The object of the summary is to derive full totals for the whole period you have been trading, which is achieved by adding the figures in each vertical column.

There will be a great many figures on the summary pages and it is easy to be intimidated. By using a calculator or adding machine it is straightforward to add the figures in each column with accuracy.

Take care not to omit a figure when you are adding the columns. If you miss, for instance, the materials total for one

MONTH	BANKED	CASH RETAINED	SALES	OTHER INCOME	
MAY	1000	200	800	400	
JUNE	600	100	500	200	
JULY	2000	100	1500	600	
AUGUST	800	100	900	—	
SEPTEMBER	1500	200	1700	—	
OCTOBER	1500	300	1800	—	
NOVEMBER	2000	500	2450	50	
DECEMBER	2500	50	2500	50	
JANUARY	2500	50	2550	—	
FEBRUARY	2000	100	2100	—	
MARCH	1500	200	1550	150	
APRIL	1000	200	950	250	
YEARLY TOTALS	18900	2100	19300	1700	

SALE OF LATHE   150
PRIVATE MONEY   1550
1700

Check Accuracy:

18900 + 2100   19300 + 1700
= 21000   = 21000

Fig. 30   Sample cash book summary – receipts

MONTH	BANK PAYMENT	CASH PAYMENT	MATERIALS	SUB-CONTRACT	TRAVEL	RENT	HEAT & LIGHT	POSTAGE & STATIONERY	SUNDRY ITEMS	CAPITAL ITEMS	DRAWINGS
MAY	1500	400	800	200	50	500	50	20	-	-	280
JUNE	1650	100	700	100	40	500	100	40	-	-	270
JULY	1500	970	800	100	50	500	-	20	100	500	400
AUGUST	1000	400	600	100	150	500	-	20	-	-	30
SEPTEMBER	1300	500	500	100	200	500	250	10	50	-	190
OCTOBER	2500	1200	800	200	-	500	-	50	50	1600	500
NOVEMBER	1500	150	500	-	100	500	200	50	-	-	300
DECEMBER	1500	150	400	100	50	500	150	-	-	-	450
JANUARY	1650	400	500	200	500	500	200	50	50	-	50
FEBRUARY	1750	300	600	200	100	500	100	200	50	-	300
MARCH	2000	50	400	-	-	500	-	100	-	400	650
APRIL	900	350	200	200	-	500	250	100	-	-	-
YEARLY TOTALS	18750	4970	6800	1500	1240	6000	1300	660	300	2500	3420

Fig. 31   Sample cash book summary – payments

month, the total that you think you have spent on materials in the whole period will be low by that amount, which may be several hundred pounds. This will cause you to pay more tax than you should!

The best way to check the accuracy of your summary is by a technique called *cross-casting* which we have already met on page 42. Take the grand total for sales and add it to those for other income. Does this new figure equal the sum of the grand totals of cash banked and cash retained? If it does then all figures have been entered on the summary correctly. If it does not then there are three things to check:

First, go back to each month and check that the totals at the bottom of the pages are correct.

Secondly, check that you have correctly transferred each monthly total to the summary page.

Thirdly, check the accuracy of the grand totals at the bottom of the summary pages. Were any monthly totals omitted?

Further analysis

Some smaller items may have had to be entered together in one column of the cash book. For instance, it is quite common to enter rent and rates together, or postage, stationery and printing. Connected items like these can remain together, but others may need re-analysis. For instance, if you ran out of columns when entering expenditures in the cash book the problem might have been temporarily solved by placing entries in the column marked sundry expenditure. If you resorted to this solution, it may now be necessary to re-analyse them in the summary. For example, your grand total for sundry expenditure in the year may include tools, subscriptions, protective clothing and canteen sundries.

If this is the case, check back through the pages of the cash book. If there are any items which you think should be distinguished in the summary, then make a note below the appropriate column. This is best explained by example

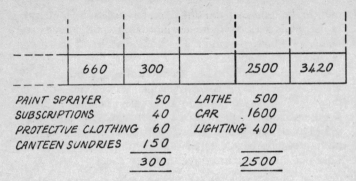

	660	300			2500	3420

PAINT SPRAYER	50	LATHE	500
SUBSCRIPTIONS	40	CAR	1600
PROTECTIVE CLOTHING	60	LIGHTING	400
CANTEEN SUNDRIES	150		
	300		2500

Fig. 32   Analysing the sundry items and capital items totals

(Fig. 32). The same procedure should be followed in re-analysing sundry receipts.

The purpose of it all

With the completion of the cash book summary it is possible to see the purpose behind book-keeping. It is condensation. The hurly-burly of everyday transactions is gradually converted to a neat set of totals which are written on just one line of the cash book – the year's totals at the bottom of the summary.

Statement of income and expenditure

Once the cash book is summarised it is possible to produce an account. The simplest form this can take is what is known as a *statement of income and expenditure*. This is not difficult as it merely involves rewriting the cash book totals in a more easily-digested form.

As in every other walk of life, book-keeping has its conventions, one of which is the appearance of the statement of income and expenditure. A sample of the usual format is shown in Fig. 33.

STATEMENT OF INCOME AND EXPENDITURE
FOR THE PERIOD ENDED (ACCOUNTS DATE)

£

Income
  Sales   W

Less: Direct costs   X

  Gross profit   Y = W — X

Less: General overheads
  Various expense headings

                                                           Z

Net profit (or loss) for period   Y — Z

Fig. 33   A pro forma statement of income and expenditure

The statement of income and expenditure shows income, or sales, and the various types and amounts of expense which are incurred in making these sales.

Note that there are two profits given. The *gross profit* is the money that is left after subtracting the material and certain other costs which were actually incorporated in the products which were sold. In the case of a photographer such costs will include those for film, developing chemicals and photographic paper. Sub-contract work can also be included.

The *net profit* or *net loss* is what is left after subtracting all general expenses from the gross profit. These expenses will include motor, travel, telephone, rent and all costs which you incur by being in business but which are not actually built into the product.

That section of the statement of income and expenditure which yields the gross profit figure is sometimes known as the *trading account*. (Fig. 34).

£

Income
Sales, etc.   W

Less: Direct costs

Materials
Sub-contract

     X

Gross profit   Y

Fig. 34   The trading account

The fixed asset schedule

This fearsome title should not be a cause of worry. It is merely a second sheet of paper on which is recorded all fixed assets, or capital items. There are generally three types, motor vehicles, plant and equipment and furniture and fittings.

Motor vehicles is self-explanatory. The heading includes every motor car, van or motorcycle which is used solely or partially for business.

Plant and equipment means any heavy or expensive piece of equipment, or tool, which is essential for the business and which will last for several years. They may be distinguished from loose tools by rule of thumb and common sense. If the equipment is quite expensive, is fairly immovable and will last for some time, then it is a "capital item". For example, a lathe comes under plant and equipment, whereas a screwdriver should be categorised as a loose tool. This is straightforward.

There are some pieces of equipment which are more difficult to place. For instance, should a typewriter be treated as plant and equipment, or as a loose tool? The answer here is to decide whether the item is durable – i.e. whether it will last for some time – and whether it is expensive. In the case of the typewriter the answer "yes" can be given to both these questions, so it is reasonably safe to regard a typewriter as plant and equipment.

Furniture and fittings include fixed or semi-portable items which are essential to the business. Examples are desks, shelves, cupboards, factory or workshop lighting and so on.

When the cash book was being drawn up, capital items should have been entered in a separate column.

Now these items should be *left out* of the statement of income and expenditure account and entered instead on the fixed asset schedule. This is so that they can be treated separately by the tax authority, who will calculate allowances against their cost.

As in the case of the income and expenditure account, it is customary to write the fixed asset schedule in a certain way (Fig. 35). Record the date of purchase, a description of the item and its cost. Do not forget to record the sale price of any item sold in the same period.

	DATE OF PURCHASE	DATE OF SALE	COST PRICE	SALE PRICE
Motor vehicles				
Plant & Equipment				
Furniture & Fittings			___	___
Totals for year				
			===	===

Fig. 35   Fixed Asset Schedule

Drawing up an account

Once the cash book has been summarised it is possible to produce, step by step, a statement of income and expenditure account and a fixed asset schedule.

There is no need to prepare a separate statement of income and expenditure if the production of a full set of accounts is contemplated, since the latter will include a trading and profit and loss account. This topic is covered in a later chapter.

Compile a draft at first so that errors can be corrected. When you are satisfied with the result a neat copy can be typed.

Account headings

Write the name of the business at the top of the paper. Some businessmen, especially High Street traders, may trade under a name other than their own. For instance, "Wealden Art Products" may in fact be run by Mr. J. Smith.

If this is so then both the trading name and the name of the proprietor should be given. This is usually done by using the abbreviation T/A, which is short for "Trading As". For example:

JOHN B. SMITH T/A WEALDEN ART PRODUCTS.

It seems superfluous to mention it, but do not be tempted to add "Ltd." to the trading name. This only applies to a business which is formally registered as a limited company.

Beneath the trading name of the business, write "Statement of Income and Expenditure for the (year or months) ended (your accounting date)".

The fictitious example given below is based on the same figures as the cash book summary (Fig. 30, page 69 and Fig. 31, page 70). It will be assumed that trading was commenced a year before the accounting date, 30th April, 19XX.

The trading account

Draw in two vertical columns to the right of the sheet of paper. These will hold all the figures which will be transferred from the cash book. The right hand column will show section totals, while individual expenses totals are shown in the left hand column. This makes the account easy to read.

There is no need to worry about further splitting these columns to show pounds and pence. Pence can be disregarded at this stage and figures can be rounded up or down to the nearest pound, viz.:

£400.28 is written as £400
£395.85 is written as £396.

The first figure entered is the total value of sales made in the trading period. This is the total at the bottom of the sales column in the cash book summary.

Write *sales* on the left of the account sheet and enter the sum in the right hand column. It appears in the right hand column because it is a total in its own right.

If the business offers a service (perhaps as an architect) then "sales" is a misnomer, and *fees received* would be a better title.

To establish a gross profit, it is now necessary to subtract from the total sales all costs related directly to the product. These should have been recorded in the cash book and the summary as materials, sub-contract and so on. Their specific nature will depend on the type of business. An artist might list not only materials but picture framing and copying as relevant to the product. On the other hand, a labourer or other contractor who sells a skill rather than a product will have no such direct costs to enter.

The description of the expense is written on the left and the total transferred from the summary to the left hand column if there is more than one type of trading account expense; the sub-total of these expenses can then be added and written into the right hand column (Fig. 36).

		£
Income		
Sales		19300
Less: Direct costs		
Materials	6800	
Sub-contract	1500	
		(8300)
Gross profit		£11000

Fig. 36   The trading account

Subtract the direct costs sub-total from the sales or fees received figure to arrive at the gross profit. Write *gross profit* on the left hand side of the page.

Other expenditure

The aim is to produce a net or final profit figure. Having derived a gross profit it is now time to list all other types of expenditure and subtract them.

Turn to the cash book summary and transfer all the totals to the account sheet, listing them vertically. The type of expenditure (i.e. telephone, postage and stationery, etc.) is written on the left and the figure entered in the left hand column, as in Fig. 37.

	£	£
Gross profit		11000
Less: General overheads		
Travel	1240	
Rent of workshop	6000	
Heat and lighting	1300	
Postage and stationery	660	
Sundry items	300	

Fig. 37   Entering general overheads

Do not enter the totals in the bank payment and cash payment columns. These were recorded to help show how the payment was made. Here we are concerned only with where the money went.

Also ignore the drawings and capital items totals at this stage. Capital items are listed separately. Drawings are relevant only to a full set of accounts (see Chapter 8, page 138).

Work steadily across the cash book summary, transferring each total to the account until they are all listed.

Add the general overheads totals, entering the result in the right hand column.

Now subtract this figure from the *gross profit* to give a *net profit* figure (Fig. 38).

The net profit represents the money left in the business after paying all relevant expenses. This is the figure upon

	£	£
Gross profit		11000
Less: General overheads		
Travel	1240	
Rent or workshop	6000	
Heat and lighting	1300	
Postage and stationery	660	
Sundry items	300	
		(9500)
Net profit		£1500

Fig. 38   Deriving a net profit

which the Tax Inspector will assess any tax which may be owed, so it is important to get it right. Go back and check your calculations to ensure that they are correct.

Partial expenses

Before we leave the subject of entering expenses we should

look at *partial expenses*. These are expenses which are not entirely incurred by the business. Two obvious examples are telephone charges and motor expenses. Very often telephones and vehicles are used for private purposes as well as business. The Tax Inspector is unlikely to allow a claim for the whole expense to be offset against tax. Probably a proportion (usually expressed as a fraction or percentage) will be allowed.

Calculate roughly how much was spent for business purposes and estimate the percentage to be entered on the account.

Take the grand total from the cash book summary, apply the percentage and enter the resulting figure on the account sheet.

For example, if in the year £1,240 has been spent on vehicle costs, but you estimate that only ¾ of the costs relate to business, then ¾ of £1,240, £930, will be the figure to include.

Show that this has been done by writing the percentage or fraction used beside the expenses heading (Fig. 39) together with a note of the full amount.

	£
Travel (75% × 1240)	930

Fig. 39   Partial expenses

Declarations

If the account is to be presented to the Inland Revenue, then the Tax Inspector will require a signature to confirm the accuracy of the accounts. It is after all an official declaration of your income and expenditure.

This is best done by means of a declaration written at the bottom of the account. Suitable wording is as follows:

"I confirm that the above account reflects an accurate picture of my financial affairs for the period ended (date) and that I have made available all relevant information.

(Signed)

Date

An example of a complete statement of income and expenditure complete with declaration is given in Fig. 40.

When the draft has been completed and checked for accuracy, produce a final typed copy.

Fixed asset schedule

There is no calculation involved in preparing a fixed asset schedule. It is merely a list of the capital items which were ignored when preparing the statement of income and expenditure.

Take a fresh sheet of paper and prepare a draft.

The title should include both your own and your business name if you have one, followed by the phrase: Fixed Asset Schedule for the (year or period) ended (date).

Refer back to the cash book summary and make a list of any motor vehicles, plant and equipment and furniture and fittings that have been brought into the business.

Record briefly what they were and what you paid on the schedule (Fig. 41). The example given uses the same figures given as examples in the section on summarising the cash book on pages 69/70, Figs. 30 and 31. For the sake of completeness we will assume that the lathe which was purchased in July for £500 was sold in March for £150 (see Fig. 30). This was treated as sundry income in the cash book.

JOHN B. SMITH

T/A WEALDEN ART PRODUCTS

*Statement of income and expenditure
for the year ended 30th April, 19XX*

	£	£
Income		
Sales		19300
Less: Direct costs		
Materials	6800	
Sub-contract	1500	
		(8300)
GROSS PROFIT		11000
Less: General overheads		
Travel (75% × 1240)	930	
Rent of workshop	6000	
Heat and lighting	1300	
Postage and stationery	660	
Sundry items	300	
		(9190)
NET PROFIT		£1810

I confirm that the above accounts reflect an accurate picture of my financial affairs for the year ended 30th April, 19XX, and that I have made available all relevant information.

Signed:

Dated:

Fig. 40   A full statement of income and expenditure

JOHN B. SMITH

T/A WEALDEN ART PRODUCTS

Fixed Asset Schedule for the year ended 30th April, 19XX

	DATE OF PURCHASE	DATE OF SALE	COST PRICE	SALE PRICE
Motor vehicles			£	£
Car – Ford Escort XYZ 123 R	20 October	—	1600	—
Plant & Equipment				
Lathe	12 July	10 March	500	(150)
Furniture & Fittings				
Workshop lighting	2 March	—	400	—
			£2500	£(150)

Fig. 41   Fixed Asset Schedule

Depreciation

Over a period of time an asset loses its value. After several years, a motor car, for instance, may only be worth a fraction of its original price. Eventually a point is reached where the car or equipment is worthless and must be discarded, or *written off*.

This decline in an asset's value is called *depreciation*. While the concept is simple, accurate calculation of depreciation can be complicated. The topic has therefore been ignored in this book. Leave calculation of depreciation to an accountant, or the Tax Inspector to whom the accounts are submitted.

When you are happy with the draft fixed asset schedule, produce a final typed copy.

It is wise to take several photocopies of completed accounts, both for safety reasons lest the original be lost or destroyed, and so that both you, the Tax Inspector and possibly the bank manager can retain a copy.

Submitting accounts

Once the statement of income and expenditure account and the fixed asset schedule have been produced submit them to the tax authorities.

They should be accompanied by a short letter explaining that you have completed your accounts for the year (or period) and would be pleased to receive the Tax Inspector's approval.

Provided that the accounts accurately reflect your financial affairs, they will probably be accepted. However, the Tax Inspector is within his rights to query the accounts or even to ask to examine your records, so keep your cash book, receipts and other records handy so that you are prepared. You need to keep them for at least six years.

6

Accounting for VAT

Value Added Tax (or VAT) is a tax levied on most business transactions in the United Kingdom and the Isle of Man, and applies (with variations) throughout the E.E.C.

Whether or not a business needs to register for VAT depends on whether the anticipated *turnover* exceeds a threshold stated from time to time by the government. In 1989/90 the threshold was an anticipated turnover of £23,600. This figure has tended to rise in line with inflation. Failure to register for VAT if your turnover is above the threshold can lead to penalties under the law.

Details of the regulations governing the collection of VAT are beyond the scope of this book. Consult the Customs and Excise office nearest you if you have any doubts about whether to register.

The maintenance of VAT records and the submission of VAT return forms can be a headache, especially for the new businessman. Yet the task is very simple if approached in the right way.

What is VAT?

Value Added Tax is a tax which is added onto the purchase price of a product or service. The rate or rates are decided and can be altered by the government. In 1989 there was a single positive rate of 15 pence in the pound (15%), which is used in all the examples in this chapter.

There are three categories of tax liability.

Rated goods

These are goods or services which are subject to the tax.

Zero rated goods

Goods or services on the sale of which VAT is charged but at a nil rate. A change in VAT regulations can alter their status.

Exempt goods

Goods or services to which VAT does not apply at all.

As the addition of VAT to the purchase price of an item increases its cost considerably, many essential goods (for instance food) or services (electricity for example) are not taxed.

Luxury goods are generally all subject to VAT.

How does VAT work?

Each time a product is sold or service rendered by a VAT registered business, VAT is added to the price at the prevailing rate. At the same time, the business is permitted to claim back VAT which it has paid on goods or services purchased. The difference between the two is either paid to or received from the Customs and Excise, depending on which sum is larger.

If more VAT is received on sales *(outputs)* than has been spent on purchases *(inputs)*, then the business has a tax surplus which must be paid to the Customs and Excise.

Should purchase (input) VAT exceed VAT received on outputs, then the business claims a refund of the balance.

How VAT is paid at each stage of production

Let us illustrate the process by following a dining room table through its various stages of manufacture and sale.

The first step in production is the purchase of rough-hewn timber from which the carpenter will work. Let us suppose he selects sufficient timber to make the table for a price of, say, £20. He must also pay VAT at 15%.

VAT at 15% on £20 = £3.

Once inside the carpenter's workshop, the rough timber is processed into the finished table, which is then offered to a wholesaler at £160. The carpenter, as a VAT registered businessman, will have to add VAT at 15% to the sale.

VAT at 15% on £160 = £24.

So the full price asked will be £160 + £24 = £184. At the same time, the carpenter can claim back the £3 VAT he paid when purchasing the timber from the sawmill:

Carpenter's VAT: Output VAT = £24
Input VAT = £ 3

Balance owed to Customs & Excise £21

The wholesaler who buys the table will advertise his stock to the retail trade. Suppose that in order to cover his costs and make a profit, he offers the table for sale at £200. VAT must be added to this price, so the wholesaler will receive £200 plus VAT, or £230:

VAT at 15% on £200 = £30

At the same time, the wholesaler can claim back the £24 VAT he paid on his purchase price of the table:

Wholesaler's VAT: Output VAT = £30
Input VAT = £24

Balance due to Customs & Excise £ 6

The retailer in turn might offer the table for sale in his shop at £300.

VAT at 15% on £300 = £45

The retailer will receive £45 VAT when he makes the sale, but does not owe the full amount to Customs and Excise. Once again, input tax paid when he bought the table can be reclaimed.

Retailer's VAT: **Output VAT = £45**
                                Input VAT = £30

Balance due to Customs & Excise   **£15**

The customer forms the end of the chain. He or she pays the full £45 tax on the final price for the table of £345 (£300 + VAT). The various transactions are shown in Fig. 42.

	CHARGED	WAS CHARGED	AMOUNT DUE TO CUSTOMS & EXCISE
Sawmill	£3		£3
Carpenter	£24	£3	£21
Wholesaler	£30	£24	£6
Retailer	£45	£30	£15
Customer	—	£45	—
			£45

Fig. 42   VAT chargeable in a string of transactions

The total amount the Customs and Excise receive at the different stages is always the same as the amount of VAT charged in the final selling price.

When you are quoting for a job, make sure it is understood that the price does not include VAT. Tax must be added to the contracted price as a separate item, otherwise you will have to pay tax due out of the sale price, thus reducing your profit margin.

Possible advantages of VAT registration

Registration is compulsory if turnover is over the threshold.

But if it is not, it may still be advantageous to apply to register voluntarily. The advantage of being registered is that VAT paid on inputs can be claimed back. The non-registered business, like the man in the street, cannot reclaim the VAT it has paid.

If your turnover is below the threshold, you should consider voluntary registration only if circumstances like the following apply:

Either your main customers are registered for VAT, and need a VAT invoice from you to claim the tax back themselves.

Or your outputs are mainly zero rated goods (or exports which are all zero rated), so that you will be in the position of reclaiming, rather than paying VAT.

But remember that being registered for VAT will cause you extra work and book-keeping. Do not register voluntarily unless it is really worthwhile.

The VAT return

Once a business is registered for VAT, the interval at which returns are to be made is decided between the trader and the Customs and Excise.

The usual periods are monthly or quarterly. The choice is based on two factors. It is more convenient to do the paperwork four times a year rather than every month, so quarterly returns are generally preferable.

However, if the business is such that repayment of tax by Customs and Excise is the norm, then it may be preferable to make declarations and receive these payments monthly.

Filling in a VAT return is straightforward. At the end of each period a certain amount of tax has been charged out to customers as part of the sale prices of the business's goods or services. (This is known as output tax. An easy way to remember is to regard sales as goods put *out* by the business.)

In the same period tax has been charged by suppliers in addition to the purchase price of materials, goods and services. This tax can in most cases be reclaimed and is known as input tax (a tax on goods flowing *into* the business).

If the tax received on sales, or output tax, is greater than the tax paid on purchases, then the business must pay the balance.

If the reverse is true, then there is money owing to the business and the balance may be claimed from the Customs and Excise.

Examples of the two situations are given in Fig. 43.

(a) Output tax (VAT charged on sales)	£2000
Less: Input tax (VAT paid on purchases)	£1000
Balance payable to Customs & Excise	£1000
(b) Output tax (VAT charged on sales)	£1000
Less: Input tax (VAT paid on purchases)	£2000
Balance to be reclaimed	£(1000)

Fig. 43   Two VAT returns: (a) Tax owed
(b) Tax owing

VAT and book-keeping

When planning a cash book for a business which *is* VAT registered, space for the VAT element must be allowed.

Also the customer can require to have a "VAT invoice" which is similar to an ordinary one which was described on page 44, Fig. 14. The VAT invoice should clearly display the VAT registration number which is issued to a VAT registered business. Also, VAT, if applicable, should be calculated at the rate in force at the time and added to the sub-total of the invoice. (Fig. 44).

VAT No 006532

AMOS & Co
TIMBER MERCHANTS
Address

2 February 19XX

TO: *Mr BROWN*   *INVOICE No: 0000*

	VAT		NET	
GOODS				
40m. 10cm.sq. Pine	15	—	100	—
20m HARDBOARD	7	50	50	—
NET GOODS TOTAL			150	—
VAT TOTAL			22	50
TOTAL AMOUNT DUE			172	50

Fig. 44   The VAT invoice

The VAT cash book

When planning the cash book, extra columns should be included for VAT received on sales and VAT paid out on purchases.

This is most important. Although the VAT need not be included in any statement of income and expenditure produced, it is essential to have a clear record. It will be needed in order to prepare VAT returns, as proof for the VAT inspector, and as an aid to the accountant if a full set of accounts is prepared.

Receipts page with VAT

The receipts page (Fig. 10, page 38) of the cash book showed where money comes from and how it is kept. There are a basic seven columns.

However, if sales are subject to VAT, and VAT is charged on top of the actual price of the item, then it would be false to record the total cash received for the sale under sales. Some of the cash will be VAT. This should be recorded separately, so an eighth column is inserted onto the page, between cash retained and sales, entitled VAT received. (Fig. 45).

		RECEIPTS PAGE				
DATE	SOURCE OR DESCRIPTION	BANKED	CASH RETAINED	VAT RECEIVED	SALES	OTHER INCOME

Fig. 45 The VAT column in the cash book – receipts

The basic sale price of the item excluding VAT is written in the sales column.

If any VAT was received for a sale, this is recorded in the VAT column.

The total cash received, which includes the VAT element, is placed in either cash retained or bank receipts, depending on whether the money was kept as cash, or banked.

Items of sundry income will probably not incur VAT, but if they do, then record VAT in the same way.

Let us suppose that an item has been sold for £200 + VAT. This means that if the VAT rate is 15% then the sum of money the customer actually paid was £200 + (15% of £200) or £200 + £30 = £230.

Of this £230, £200 was the real price and £30 was the VAT element.

When recording the transaction in the cash book, first write in the date of payment and the name of the buyer.

The total sum received for that sale is then recorded in the cash banked or cash retained columns as appropriate.

The net amount of the sale, that is, the original sale price, is written in the sales column.

		RECEIPTS PAGE				
DATE	SOURCE OR DESCRIPTION	BANKED	CASH RETAINED	VAT RECEIVED	SALES	OTHER INCOME
10th FEBRUARY	SALES	230.00		30.00	200.00	
15th FEBRUARY	SALES	100.00			100.00	
20th FEBRUARY	GIFT		20.00			20.00

Fig. 46   Entering receipts with VAT element

If the sale was not subject to VAT (as in the second and third transactions in Fig. 46), then there is none to record. But if it was, enter the amount of VAT in the VAT received column.

Payments page with VAT

VAT on payments which are made should be recorded as follows:

NET GOODS TOTAL	150	—
VAT TOTAL	22	50
TOTAL AMOUNT DUE	172	50

Fig. 47 Totals on a VAT invoice

Study the invoice you have paid. Three groups of figures appear (Fig. 47), although they may be in different positions on computerised invoices. These are:

(1) The net amount which was paid for the items.
(2) The VAT.
(3) The full total, including VAT.

These three figures should be entered separately in the cash book under their respective headings. To accomplish this you need an extra "VAT" column as shown in Fig. 48. The other columns are the same as in Fig. 17, page 49.

DATE	SUPPLIER OR DESCRIPTION	CHQ No.	BANK PAYMENT	CASH PAYMENT	VAT PAID	MATERIALS
			PAYMENTS			

Fig. 48   The VAT column in the cash book – payments

DATE	SUPPLIER OR DESCRIPTION	CHQ No.	BANK PAYMENT	CASH PAYMENT	VAT PAID	MATERIALS
			PAYMENTS			
2nd FEBRUARY	TIMBER	562	115.00		15.00	100.00
3rd FEBRUARY	GOODS			20.00	—	20.00

Fig. 49   Entering up the VAT cash book – payments

When you record a payment which has included VAT write the total paid (including VAT) into either the bank or cash payment column as appropriate.

Insert into the VAT paid column the VAT element which appears on the bill.

Place the net price (excluding VAT) under whichever column is relevant, e.g. materials (Fig. 49).

If you pay a bill which carries no VAT, record the total paid in either the bank or cash payment column, and again under the appropriate expense heading. Leave the VAT column blank.

Summarising the VAT cash book

At the end of each month add the entries in each column and write the total at the bottom of the page. Do this for both receipts and payments.

Check for accuracy.

On the receipts page, cash banked + cash retained should equal VAT received + sales + other income.

On the payments page, bank payments + cash payment should equal VAT paid plus the sum of all the analysis columns (Fig. 50).

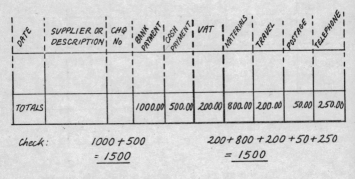

DATE	SUPPLIER OR DESCRIPTION	CHQ No	BANK PAYMENT	CASH PAYMENT	VAT	MATERIALS	TRAVEL	POSTAGE	TELEPHONE
TOTALS			1000.00	500.00	200.00	800.00	200.00	50.00	250.00

Check: 1000 + 500   200 + 800 + 200 + 50 + 250
        = 1500   = 1500

Fig. 50   Sample monthly summary – cash book payments

If these figures do not balance then check the calculations of the totals, and the entries to make sure that no mistakes have been made and no entries left out.

The end of year summary of the cash book is produced in exactly the same way as was shown in Chapter 4. There will be two extra columns to add, VAT received on sales and VAT paid out on purchases.

The VAT summary – the cash accounting scheme

VAT is usually accounted for on the basis of the tax invoices you issue and receive. However, some small businesses are allowed to account for their VAT under the cash accounting scheme. These businesses still have to issue and keep tax invoices and keep all the normal records required by Customs and Excise, but under this scheme they account for their VAT on the basis of the actual *payments* they receive and make. Their VAT return is therefore completed by using the figures contained in their VAT cash book.

If you wish to use the cash accounting scheme, contact Customs and Excise for more details.

A VAT summary has to be made every time a VAT return is complete. This may sound intimidating but is in fact very simple. The basis of the VAT return is:

Tax received on outputs *minus* tax paid on inputs *equals* balance.

If the amount received is greater than that paid out, then the balance is payable to the Customs and Excise.

If the VAT paid out in the period is greater than that received, then a rebate may be claimed.

Total VAT received in period (output VAT)	☐	X
Total VAT paid in period (input VAT)	☐	Y
Balance	☐	X – Y
Total net outputs in period	☐	
Total net inputs in period	☐	

Fig. 51 Form of VAT summary – monthly

To record details of VAT totals, take a clean page at the back of the cash book, and entitle it "VAT summaries". Summarise the receipts and payments pages. The total VAT received in the month will be the total of the VAT column on the receipts page. The total VAT paid will be the equivalent total on the payments page. Transfer the VAT totals to the VAT summary. (Fig. 51.)

Subtract one from the other and record the balance. This will be the sum which you must pay or claim for the month.

If you are doing monthly returns, simply transfer these figures to the appropriate boxes on the VAT return form which will have been sent by the Customs and Excise.

If quarterly returns are made, summarise three months together as in Fig. 52.

The two other pieces of information required on the VAT return are "value of outputs" for the period and "value of inputs".

These are simply the total of receipts and payments which were subject to VAT.

They are derived by adding the total of the "sales" columns for outputs, and the total of the analysis columns for inputs.

Do not include items which are exempt from VAT such as rents, rates, wages, and personal payments, or drawings. (The VAT element in private payments cannot be reclaimed.)

Record the result in the boxes indicated on the VAT return.

The completed form is submitted to Customs and Excise, either enclosing payment of the balance or asking for a refund.

The VAT summary – the non-cash accounting scheme

If you do not want to use the cash accounting scheme or Customs and Excise do not allow you to use it, then you have to account for the VAT on the basis of your sales invoices and not the money actually received. A firm may

Total VAT received in period (output VAT)

Month A [   ]

B [   ]

C [   ]

[   ] subtotal X

Total VAT paid in period (input VAT)

Month A [   ]

B [   ]

C [   ]

[   ] subtotal Y

[   ] X – Y

BALANCE

Value of net outputs in period:
Month A [   ]

B [   ]

C [   ]

[   ]

Value of net inputs in period:

Month A [   ]

B [   ]

C [   ]

[   ]

Fig. 52   Form of VAT summary – quarterly

invoice £2,000 worth of sales in a month, but only receive (say) £1,500. But the amount to be taken into account for VAT is the full £2,000.

If you do not use the cash accounting scheme, you fill in the VAT form by using the figures contained in your *sales day book*.

The sales day book is very easy to prepare. It is drawn up in exactly the same way as the receipts page of the cash book. The difference is that the sales day book records the amounts invoiced during the month, and not the actual cash received. The information to include is similar: the name of each client, the date of the invoice, the gross figure invoiced, the VAT element, and the net value of the sale.

At the end of each VAT period, the columns are totalled. The total in the VAT column is then transferred to the VAT return form.

The sales day book is kept in a separate book, or on sheets drawn up for the purpose.

For small firms, the input VAT (deductible from total VAT liability) can be derived by totalling the VAT column in the cash book each month/quarter as above, but larger firms or those which receive regular VAT refunds would use a *purchase day book* in which each incoming invoice is set down according to its date of issue (tax point).

Payments to Customs and Excise

Care must be taken to distinguish between the VAT columns in the cash book and payments to, or receipts from, Customs and Excise.

The VAT columns are a record of the VAT received from sales or paid on purchases.

Money actually paid to or received from the Customs and Excise is a separate payment or receipt arising from completion and submission of the VAT return.

Record receipts from the Customs and Excise under a separate heading of that name or include it amongst sundry income, making a note of what it was.

Payments to Customs and Excise should have a separate

column on the payments page; if there is no space, they should be included in sundry payments, with a note beside the figure.

The figure is then entered again in the bank or cash columns as appropriate. These items should NOT be included in the calculation of later VAT returns.

Retailers

If you are a retailer, contact the Customs and Excise for details of retailers' special schemes.

Good advice

This chapter is intended as a working guide to the maintenance of VAT records. It is important that Customs and Excise are consulted about your specific circumstances.

7

Club Accounts

Basic book-keeping skills are essential to the Treasurer of a Club, Society or Association.

He is responsible to the members of the Club for maintaining proper records, keeping track of money paid in, and how the money is spent. In many ways a Club or Society can be regarded as a small business, and the requirements for keeping a proper record are similar.

A basic difference is that the bulk of a Society's income may come from members' subscriptions. These, rather than sales, will probably be the prime source of finance.

Bank accounts

Unless the Club is very small indeed, open a separate bank account for it with its own paying in book and cheque book.

Recording subscriptions and donations

Some clubs have an annual subscription. Others, for instance small sports clubs, have a weekly payment.

The Treasurer must ensure that a complete list of members' names is available. By recording accurately what each member owes, any controversy can be quickly solved.

Where *annual subscriptions* are demanded, the book-keeping is simple.

Draw up a list of members on a sheet of paper. Then, across the top of the sheet, write in columns for dates of payment, amount due, amount received and a column for any balance outstanding. It is useful to add a sundry or donations column. A member might for example make an extra donation which should be recorded. (Fig. 53).

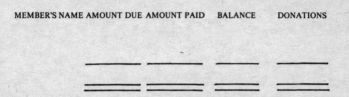

MEMBER'S NAME AMOUNT DUE AMOUNT PAID   BALANCE   DONATIONS

Fig. 53   Club subscriptions register – annual subs.

As each member's subscription is received, the amount is entered in the amount paid column, together with a note of the date. If less or more than the right amount (recorded in the amount due column) is paid, then the balance outstanding is recorded under the balance heading. It is useful to establish a simple code so that no confusion arises. If the balance indicates that the money was overpaid, then the balance could either be written in red, or alternatively written in brackets. These are two common book-keeping codes for minus figures and come in handy when calculating the total balance owed or owing. (Fig. 54).

MEMBER'S NAME	AMOUNT DUE	AMOUNT PAID	BALANCE
A J. Smith	£40	£30	£10
B J. Brown	£40	£50	(£10)

Fig. 54   Recording negative balances (in brackets)

MEMBER'S NAME	AMOUNT DUE	AMOUNT PAID	BALANCE (+ = OWING)	DONATIONS
	£	£	£	£
J. Smith	40	20	20	—
J. Brown	40	50	(10)	—
A. White	40	40	—	—
P. Jones	40	40	—	20
R. Green	40	40	—	—
Totals	£200	£190	(£10)	£20

Total receipts for year = 190 Subs
                          20 Donations
                         ─────────────
                         £210

Fig. 55   Annual subscriptions register summary

At the end of the accounting period the various columns are totalled vertically. It is then possible to see exactly how much was received, how much due, and how much is still owed for the whole year. Any extra donations can be summarised. (Fig. 55).

If a Club runs on a *weekly* basis, then subscriptions may be weekly-based provided that if a member does not turn up then he is not required to pay for that week. Then the method of accounting is still straightforward but requires a little more paper.

Across the top of a broad sheet of paper, preferably squared paper, write in the weeks, from 1 to 52. If required then a brief note can be made of what date is involved, viz. Wk. 1, Jan. 7.

Decide at the start on what date the Club requires accounts. The subscription list should run a year to that date. For instance, if, as is common, the accounts are required to the end of the month preceding the Annual

NAME	WK 1	2	3	4	5	6	7	8	9	10	11	12	13	14	15	16	17	18	19	20	ETC	TOTAL
J. SMITH		✓	✓	✓	✓	✓	✓	✓		✓	✓	✓	✓	✓	✓							13
J. BROWN	✓	✓	✓	✓	✓	✓	✓	✓	✓	✓	✓	✓	✓	✓								14

Fig. 56 Club subscriptions register – weekly records

NAME	WK 1	2	3	4	5	48	49	50	51	52	TOTAL	SUB RATE	TOTAL RECEIVED
J. SMITH	✓	✓	✓	✓			✓	✓	✓	✓	48	£4	£192
J. BROWN	✓		✓		✓	✓		✓	✓		40	4	160
A. WHITE	✓	✓	✓		✓	✓	✓	✓	✓	✓	52	4	208
P. JONES	✓		✓		✓	✓		✓	✓		40	4	160
R. GREEN	✓	✓	✓		✓	✓		✓	✓	✓	45	4	180
TOTAL RECEIVED IN YEAR											225	4	900

A TOTAL OF 225 ATTENDANCES × £4 PER WEEK = £900

Fig. 57 Weekly subscriptions register summary for year

General Meeting, then records should start a year before that date.

Some clubs may require six-monthly accounts. The process here is identical. It just means that records must be summarised more frequently.

Down the left side of the sheet write in the names of the members.

When subscriptions are collected during the session it is then a simple matter to place a tick in the appropriate square as each member pays his or her money. (Fig. 56).

Clubs that run monthly subscriptions can also run on this system, substituting the twelve months of the year for fifty-two weeks.

Where weekly or monthly records are maintained, generally the subscription rate for each week will be the same for all members. But there may be reduced rates for children or pensioners.

Add up the number of ticks which indicate a member's attendance record and multiply this total by the appropriate weekly (or monthly) subscription rate. Record the answer at the far right of the page.

When the process has been completed for every member, add the totals received from each person to give the total subscriptions received in the year. (Fig. 57).

The Club cash book

The cash book is an essential means of recording the flow of money into and out of the Club. It is similar to the cash book used by businesses, but there are differences. Ready-made cash books available in stationers are quite adequate or you can draw up cash sheets along the lines given in Chapter 4, page 35.

Receipts

These represent the money flowing into the club from subscriptions, donations and the proceeds of events, etc. We will want to distinguish between these sources, and to show where the money went after it was received. That is, whether it was paid into the Club's bank account, or kept for use as petty cash for day-to-day expenses.

With this in mind, head up the columns on the receipts page (the left hand sheet).

The first column gives the date on which money was received. The second gives details of the source of income. If money was received from a sale or bazaar then it is useful to note details of the event (in the source of income column). Donations should similarly be recorded against the name of the donor. Subscriptions will probably be collected and then paid into the bank in lump sums, in which case a note that they were subscriptions can be made. If subscriptions are recorded individually then the name of the member should be placed against the entry.

The third and fourth columns in the cash book should be entitled banked and cash retained respectively. If preferred,

		RECEIPTS					
DATE	SOURCE OF INCOME	BANKED	CASH RETAINED	SUBS	DONATIONS	EVENTS	SUNDRY INCOME
28th FEBRUARY	SUBS	300.00		300.00			
1st MARCH	SIR J. WHEELER	100.00			100.00		
31st MARCH	JUMBLE SALE	320.00	9.46			329.46	
6th APRIL	COUNCIL GRANT	150.00					150.00

Fig. 58   Club cash book – receipts page headings and entries

the cash retained column can be named petty cash or cash float.

Subsequent columns could be entitled subscriptions (subs), donations and events. A column marked sundry income is useful for any odd sums which do not fall into any other category.

As money is received, the relevant details can now be entered into the cash book (Fig. 58).

The amount is placed within the appropriate analysis column, viz. subscriptions, donations, etc., and then entered again under banked or cash retained (part into each, if only part of the money is banked).

Transfers from cash to bank

If a substantial sum is collected as cash and then paid into the bank at a later date, care is needed. The best method is not to complete the entry until you are sure how much is being paid into the bank.

Alternatively, record the receipt of the money as cash retained, and subsequently transfer the amount banked into the banked column. The figure is written into the banked column and then either crossed out in the cash retained column or a minus figure is entered, shown by drawing brackets around it. (Fig. 59). This minus figure should then

		RECEIPTS					
DATE	SOURCE OF INCOME	BANKED	CASH RETAINED	SUBS	DONATIONS	EVENTS	SUNDRY INCOME
28th FEBRUARY	SUBS	200.00	200.00	200.00			
28th FEBRUARY	SUBS	200.00	(200.00)	200.00			

Fig. 59   Cash book entries for recording cash transferred to bank

be subtracted when totalling the column. It should not be ignored as only a proportion of the cash received may be banked.

Payments

The payments page in the cash book may be drafted along similar lines to that required by a business (page 46).

Head up the vertical columns, starting with the date and then a description of what was bought.

There can then be a space to enter cheque numbers as a cross reference to the club cheque book.

It is useful to know how the payment was made, so the next two columns are entitled bank payment and cash payment.

The remaining columns in the cash book are to analyse the various categories of expense. These will differ slightly from business expenses. Materials and sub-contract costs, for instance, are unlikely to occur. A list of common expenses met by a Club might include:

Printing costs
Advertising
Telephone costs
Stall or hall rent
Postage and stationery
Wages (if full-time staff are retained)

All types of expenses paid out of Club funds should have a separate column.

At convenient intervals the cash book is brought up to date by entering every expense, with the date of payment and a description. The amount is entered twice, once under the appropriate expense column, and again under bank or cash payments as appropriate (Fig. 60).

At the end of each month the transactions, both receipts and payments, are summarised by adding the figure in each column.

| | | | | PAYMENTS | | | | | |
DATE	DESCRIPTION	CHQ No	BANK PAYMENT	CASH PAYMENT	COSTUME COSTS	HALL RENT	HEAT LIGHT	ADVERTS	POSTAGE & STATIONERY
2nd FEBRUARY	COSTUMES	234	20.00		(DIRECT COST) 20.00				
3rd FEBRUARY	JANUARY RENT			40.00		40.00			
4th FEBRUARY	KENT ECHO	235	100.00					100.00	

Fig. 60   Making cash book entries for payments

The cash book summary

At the end of the year, all the monthly totals are transferred to a summary, the procedure being the same as that given on page 66.

Annual accounts

These should be of professional appearance. They can be neatly typed and sufficient copies provided for every member of the governing committee, or even for each member of the Club, according to the Rules.

Small clubs require only a statement of income and expenditure. (If equipment or vehicles have been purchased for Club use, then you should prepare in addition a fixed asset schedule showing major items purchased and sold.)

First summarise the cash book if this has not been done already.

Take a sheet of paper and head it up with the name of the Club, the period which the account covers, and the date at which the period ends, e.g.:

Thornton Amateur Dramatic Society
Accounts for the year ended 31st December, 19XX

The first figures to transfer from the cash book summary are the various types of income.

The Club Treasurer must declare *all* types of income to his members. Transfer the year's (or half-year's) total receipts to the account, category by category. Sub-total these figures to give a total income figure. (Fig. 61).

At this stage list any types of expenses specifically incurred in carrying on the activity of the Club. These are the *direct* costs which are directly related to the functions of the Club or Society. For example, an amateur dramatic society could list among direct costs the expense of costumes and scenery. These costs would not occur if no plays were performed, whereas more general overheads such as telephone costs and stationery and postage would still arise.

THORNTON AMATEUR DRAMATIC SOCIETY

Accounts for the year ended 31st December, 19XX

	£
Income	
Ticket sales	1500
Subscriptions	1000
Donations	50
Proceeds of bazaar	100
	2650

Fig. 61   Totalling club receipts

Sub-total these direct costs (if any) and deduct them from the total income as in Fig. 62 to arrive at what should accurately be called the *gross surplus or deficit*. This figure is like the gross profit in business accounting, mentioned on page 73.

The next step is to list all other expenses which appear in the cash book, transferring the totals one by one from the cash book summary. These should then be sub-totalled and subtracted from the gross surplus or deficit to give a *net surplus or deficit*.

Any net income left at the end of the year is a reserve which remains in the bank until required. It should be noted that no satisfactory statement of bank reserves can be expressed in a simple set of accounts comprising a statement of income and expenditure and a Fixed Asset Schedule. If more sophisticated treatement is required then reference should be made to Chapter 8.

Assuming no additional funds are available to the Club, it is difficult to achieve a net loss, as this means more money was spent than received. It is possible, however, that certain payments were made by members out of their own pockets.

THORNTON AMATEUR DRAMATIC SOCIETY

Accounts for the year ended 31st December, 19XX

	£
Income	
Ticket sales	1500
Subscriptions	1000
Donations	50
Proceeds of bazaar	100
	2650
Less: Direct costs	
Costume – Twelfth Night 200	
Scenery 300	
	(500)
Gross surplus	2150

**Fig. 62   Dealing with direct costs and finding the gross
   surplus**

Accounting for fixed assets

Certain purchases which should be itemised on a separate
schedule include motor vehicles, furniture and fittings and
plant and equipment. They are called *fixed assets*; items
which are expensive and expected to function for some
years. This category might include a permanent costume
wardrobe in the case of a theatrical group, boats for a yacht
club and video equipment owned by a photographic society.

The equipment register

So that the Society knows what equipment it owns it is wise
to maintain an equipment register, which should be up-
dated every time an item is bought or sold. Information

given in the register should include a description of the asset, the date of its purchase, date of sale, its cost and the sale price, if any, should it be sold (Fig. 63).

THORNTON AMATEUR DRAMATIC SOCIETY

Equipment register for the year ended 31st December, 19XX

ASSET	PURCHASE DATE	SALE DATE	COST PRICE	SALE PRICE
Van	15th January, 19XX	—	£1500	—
Props	19th February, 19XX	20th July, 19XX	400	200
		TOTALS	£1900	£200

Fig. 63 Sample equipment register

The complete account consists of an income and expenditure account like Fig. 64, to which should be appended the equipment register (if any) and a Treasurer's Declaration.

Declarations
There is not quite the need for a Treasurer's Declaration in Club accounts as exists for the certification of business accounts. It is, however, a good idea if, having checked and re-checked the accuracy of the records, confirmation that this has been done is written into the accounts. A suitable format might be as in Fig. 65.

Possibly more common than the Treasurer's Declaration is the appointment of an Hon. Auditor. He is usually a professional person such as a Bank Manager, Solicitor or Accountant, and is appointed by the Annual General

THORNTON AMATEUR DRAMATIC SOCIETY

Accounts for the year ended 31st December, 19XX

	£
Income	
Ticket sales	1500
Subscriptions	1000
Donations	50
Proceeds of bazaar	100
	2650

Less: Direct costs		
Costume – Twelfth Night	200	
Scenery	300	
		(500)
Gross surplus		2150

Less: General expenses		
Hall rent	200	
Heat and light	100	
Advertisements/publicity	40	
Postage and stationery	80	
		(420)
Net surplus of income over expenditure for year		1730

Fig. 64   A complete income and expenditure account

Meeting to do an independent check of the accounts at the end of each year.

Where there is an Hon. Auditor, the Treasurer prepares the accounts and passes them over to the Hon. Auditor along with vouchers, bank statements, bills, etc., and it is up to the Hon. Auditor to satisfy himself that the accounts accurately reflect the transactions of the Club. He then confirms this in his own words on the financial statement which is copied and circulated to the members.

Treasurer's Declaration

These accounts have been prepared from the financial records of the Thornton Amateur Dramatic Society, and I confirm that they accurately reflect the transactions of the Club.

Signed:

Date:

Fig. 65   Treasurer's declaration

8

A full set of accounts

The statement of income and expenditure is a means of expressing concisely the result of a year's trading by a business or club, but such a simple statement leaves out many important facts.

For instance the balances on the bank and cash accounts did not appear. No place was given to the drawings figures (the sum that was taken out of the business for private purposes) nor provision made for the money introduced by way of loans, gifts or injection of private funds by the owner of the business.

The statement of income and expenditure represents the trading situation only.

So how can the additional information be expressed? The answer is with a *balance sheet*.

A full set of accounts as produced by an accountant will consist of three sheets of paper which together give practically all the required information about a business (or indeed a club). The three sheets are:

Trading and profit and loss account
Balance sheet
Fixed asset schedule

There is nothing terrifying about this trio. Indeed, we have met two of them already. The trading and profit and loss account (TPL) is the statement of income and expenditure with small differences. The fixed asset schedule too is very similar to that described on page 81.

There is no need for a self-employed craftsman, trader, or club to produce a full set of accounts. A statement of income and expenditure and simple schedule of fixed assets is all that is required.

If, however, the business is larger, with more complex affairs, it is worth learning how to compile a balance sheet as well. This is not difficult but does require a little more thought and paperwork.

In this example we will base our calculations on the figures given in Figs. 30 and 31 (pages 69 and 70), and Fig. 40 (page 82).

The balance sheet

The balance sheet gives an overall picture of what gains and losses the business is left with on one particular day – the date of the accounts. If the business has made a gain in one particular area, this is regarded as an asset. A loss in an area is called a liability.

The difference between assets and liabilities should be the same as the difference between capital injected into the business and capital taken out.

Should the bank account show a credit balance, then this is good for the business. A gain has been made. The credit balance is an *asset*.

When the opposite applies and the bank account is overdrawn, this is unhealthy, and therefore the overdrawn balance is a *liability*.

There are two sorts of asset. Fixed assets are as described on page 74. Current assets are variable and include surpluses in the bank and cash accounts, building society accounts, any stock which the business retains at the end of the year, and money owed to the business or *debtors*.

Generally there are current liabilities only. These may include overdrawn balances in the bank and cash accounts, as well as money owed to other people. The latter are called *creditors*.

By subtracting all liabilities from the sum of the assets, we can arrive at an overall balance. If liabilities are greater the balance will be negative. If assets are larger, the figure will be positive.

The capital account

The capital account is part of the balance sheet, and is generally written on the same sheet.

Obviously, to finance the various gains and losses the business has made, money must have come into the business and then flowed out again. The difference between these two movements should, if all records have been kept correctly, equal the difference between assets and liabilities.

Money will have flowed into the business as sales or as money brought in from other sources: gifts or personal investment. The injection of money from such sources is known as *capital introduced*. By adding capital introduced and any net trading profit made, we know how much money came into the business.

Money flowed out of the business in one of two ways: as a net trading loss, if one was made, or as a personal withdrawal.

The difference between the amount of money which came in and the amount that flowed out should be the same as the difference between assets and liabilities.

Because the two should balance, these calculations are collectively known as the balance sheet. (Fig. 66).

A blank balance sheet should be prepared so that each balance can be transferred as it is found.

Take a blank sheet of paper, preferably lined, and complete it as is shown in Fig. 67.

Several lines should be left between each heading so that if necessary a number of entries can be made under each and then added to find the sub-total.

There need only be space for one entry opposite Fixed

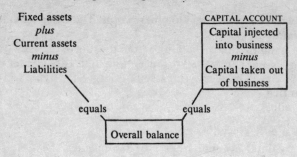

Fig. 66   The principle of the balance sheet

Fixed assets

Add: Current assets

TOTAL ASSETS

Less: Current liabilities

Capital account

Capital introduced

Net profit (if applicable)

TOTAL

Less: Drawings

Net loss (if applicable)

Fig. 67   Drafting a blank balance sheet

Assets. This figure will be the balance transferred from the fixed asset schedule.

The trading and profit and loss account (or TPL)

The first step to producing a full set of accounts is to draw up a trading and profit and loss account.

The method is practically identical to that given for producing a statement of income and expenditure account. Refer to Chapter 5 (page 72) for detailed instructions. The example used is given in Fig. 40, page 82.

There is one difference. Certain additions may be made to the draft at a later stage, so ensure that there is space for at least two entries against each heading.

Head the draft TPL with the trading name of the business and "Trading and Profit and Loss account for the Year (or period) ended (insert the accounting date)".

Under the heading are listed sales, direct costs and general expenses. At the bottom of the page will appear the net profit, or loss, which results from subtracting expenses from sales.

If the result is a net trading loss, then the figure should be bracketed to make it clear that it is a minus figure, thus:

Net trading loss   £(476)

If the business is subject to VAT registration and VAT is accounted for in the cash book, it is important to note that payments to and receipts from the Customs and Excise should not be included as an expense or receipt on the TPL. They should be ignored at this stage, as they will be dealt with later as a part of the balance sheet.

As in Chapter 5, the following columns in the cash book should be ignored when preparing the TPL:

Gifts received
Bank receipts totals
Cash receipts totals
Fixed assets sold

Bank payments total
Cash payments total
VAT transactions with Customs and Excise
Personal withdrawals
Fixed assets bought and sold
Stock

Stock, which is surplus material or products which have not been used or sold by the end of the accounting period, was omitted in Chapter 5 as it does not relate strictly to the trading gains and losses made by the business. However, if a full set of accounts is to be drawn up stock should be accounted for. How to deal with it is explained on page 132.

Reconciling the bank account

The purpose of reconciling the bank account is to check the accuracy of the records contained in the cash book and to confirm the balance in the bank at the date on which the accounts are prepared. Most of this work should have been done at the time the bank statements arrived (in order to check them!), but if not, proceed as follows:

First, collect all bank statements received during the year. Make sure they are all there, including the last one received, which should overshoot the accounting date. If one is missing, order a replacement from the bank.

Let us suppose the business has just finished its first period of trading. Every time a cheque was made out for a purchase, the amount should have been entered in the cash book under bank payments, together with the cheque number. Find the corresponding entry on the statement. If the two agree tick both figures, the one in the cash book and the one in the bank statement, using a coloured ball-point or pencil.

Proceed to the next entry in the cash book and repeat the process. Continue until all items in the cash book which were paid by cheque have been ticked. Check to ensure none have been missed.

Some entries in the payments column of the bank statement may remain unticked. These are probably standing orders, bank charges, interest or bounced cheques that were omitted when compiling the cash book. If so, enter these figures onto the cash book summary. They should appear twice, once in the bank payments column and again under the appropriate analysis column – e.g. bank charges and interest. Standing orders will be for a specific category of expense, such as insurance, and should be entered under that heading, as well as the bank payments column.

Tick these extra entries on bank statements and in the cash book.

If all has gone well, all payments in the bank statements and bank payments in the cash book should now be ticked. The more carefully the cash book was prepared, the easier it is to agree the figures on the bank statement.

This process can now be repeated with the receipts. The first entry on the receipts page of the cash book shown as having been banked should also appear on the bank statement. If it does, then tick them both. Repeat the procedure for all receipts in the period.

If a receipt appears in the bank statement but is missing from the cash book because you forgot to enter it, the amount should be added to the cash book summary (receipts page) as a correction, noting it twice – once under banked and again under the appropriate analysis column. Tick the correction and the bank statement entry.

Cheques sometimes take some while to be processed, especially if the recipients are slow paying them in. If a cheque is drawn shortly before the accounting date, it may not appear on the bank statement until after that date, in which case it is *outstanding*. It should not be ticked, but instead marked o/s, as an abbreviation for outstanding.

The same procedure should be followed if any bank receipts are outstanding.

Take a sheet of paper and write Bank Reconciliation and the date at the top.

First record the balance shown on the bank statement at the accounting date.

Next examine the cash book for any outstanding cheques or receipts. List all items marked o/s on the draft bank reconciliation and sub-total them.

If the balance indicates an overdraft (e.g. if it is marked DR.) then the outstanding cheques will make this balance larger. If the account is in credit then the balance will be reduced.

The logic of this should be apparent. But if it is not, do not worry. Just consult the following table:

Bank account in credit   *Subtract o/s cheques –*
                                 Add o/s receipts
Bank account overdrawn   *Add o/s cheques –*
                                 Subtract o/s receipts

This will give the true balance at the end of the accounting period. (Fig. 68).

BANK RECONCILIATION

		£
Balance per bank statement		204.00
Add: Outstanding receipts	92.00	
	35.00	
	40.00	
		167.00
		371.00
Subtract: Outstanding cheques	100.00	
	25.00	
	96.00	
		(221.00)
True bank balance		£150.00

The instructions to add and subtract would be reversed if the bank balance was overdrawn.

Fig. 68   Deriving the true bank balance

The true balance should also be the difference between all bank receipts and payments in the year or accounting period. Every item on the bank statement should be duplicated by the cash book, and it was to confirm this fact that entries in both were ticked to one another.

It follows that by subtracting the bank payments total which is given by the cash book summary from the total bank receipts, the resulting difference should be the same as the true balance which we have derived from the bank statements. (Fig. 69).

BANK RECONCILIATION

		£
Balance per bank statement		204.00
Add: Outstanding receipts	92.00	
	35.00	
	40.00	
		167.00
		371.00
Subtract: Outstanding cheques	100.00	
	25.00	
	96.00	
		(221.00)
True bank balance		£150.00
Cash book agreement		
Opening balance		NIL
Total banked (see Fig. 30)		18900.00
Less: Total bank payments (see Fig. 31)		(18750.00)
		£150.00

Fig. 69   Checking bank balance to cash book

Enter this true bank balance on the blank balance sheet.

Be sure to enter it under the correct heading. If there is money in the bank it is a current asset. An overdraft should be listed as a current liability. (Fig. 70).

	£	£
Fixed assets		
Current assets		
Bank balance	150	
Current liabilities		
[Bank overdraft	150]	

The entry in square brackets would be made if the bank account was overdrawn.

Fig. 70   Entering the bank balance on the balance sheet

Carrying forward the balance

If a bank reconciliation is being prepared for a second or subsequent year of trading, the reconciliation must be adjusted for the balance left in the bank account at the end of the previous year.

A nil opening balance as shown in Fig. 69 would only apply in the first year of trading. In later periods, the true bank balance at the start of the year's trading should be inserted (Fig. 71), so that the bank reconciliation agrees.

CASH BOOK AGREEMENT

		£	
Opening bank balance		950.00	[(950.00)]
Add: Total banked	18900.00		
Total bank payments	(18750.00)		
		150.00	
		£1100.00	[(800.00)]

The entries in square brackets would apply if the opening bank balance was overdrawn.

Fig. 71   Agreeing the bank balance in subsequent years

The cash account balance

Probably some payments were made in cash and some receipts were also kept as cash, i.e. not paid into the bank.

The difference between cash retained and cash paid out is a balance, and should be recorded on the balance sheet.

If more cash was received than spent, then the balance is positive. We are left with cash-in-hand, which is an asset.

Should cash payments exceed cash received then there is a problem. Banks may allow overdrafts, but in the case of cash you cannot spend more than you have in the business. So you have introduced some of your personal money to cover the additional expenses. The balance should therefore be regarded as capital introduced, and recorded as such in the capital account portion of the balance sheet.

To find the balance on the cash account, take the grand total of the cash payments column on the cash book summary and deduct the figure from the grand total of the cash retained column. The difference is the cash account balance. (Fig. 72).

	£	£
(a) *Fixed assets*		
Current assets		
Bank balance	150.00	
[Cash account balance	2870.00]	
Current liabilities		‾‾‾‾
		════
(b) *Capital account*		
Capital introduced		2870.00
Net profit (if applicable)		
Drawings		
Net loss (if applicable)		
	‾‾‾‾	‾‾‾‾
		════

If the balance on the cash account is positive (i.e. cash remains in the business), the balance is an asset (a).

If more cash was spent than received, then the balance should be recorded as capital introduced (b).

Fig. 72 Treatment of the cash account balance

The VAT balance

It was said in the section on drawing up the TPL (page 121) that payments and receipts involving VAT and Customs and Excise should not be entered at that stage.

This is because they are not strictly related to trading. A receipt of a VAT refund is not a sale, and a payment of tax due is not a direct expense of the business.

The difference between VAT received and VAT paid is, however, a genuine balance. If at the end of the year the business is owed money by the VAT account then this is an asset and it is money the business should receive in due course.

If the business owes VAT to the Customs and Excise, then this is a liability as the money will soon be paid out.

To find the balance on the VAT account, follow the guide in Fig. 73.

	PAID OUT £	RECEIVED £
Output VAT (from cash book summary or sales day book)		☐
Input VAT (from cash book summary)	☐	
VAT paid over to Customs & Excise in year	☐	
VAT repayments received from Customs & Excise in year		☐

	Balance owed		Balance owing
Difference (either)	☐	OR	☐
	☐	*is the same as*	☐

Fig. 73   VAT account guide

From the cash book summary extract the totals in the VAT columns, one for VAT received on sales and the other for VAT included in purchases and write them into the spaces shown. (But if yours is not a cash business, then get these figures from the sales and perhaps purchase day books.)

Examine the sundry receipts column for the whole period (or Customs and Excise column if there was one) to ascertain how much (if any) was received from Customs and Excise.

Examine the sundry payments, or Customs and Excise payments column for payments to the Customs and Excise. Fill the total in where shown.

The balance will be the difference between the two columns. See below how to know whether this balance is an asset or liability and record it on the blank balance sheet.

Asset = *Balance owed to business*
Liability = *Balance owed by business*

A sample VAT account is given in Fig. 74.

	PAID OUT	RECEIVED
	£	£
Output VAT		
(from cash book summary or sales day book)		1000
Input VAT		
(from cash book summary)	500	
VAT paid over to Customs & Excise in year	400	
VAT repayments received from Customs & Excise in year		100
Balance owed to Customs and Excise	200	
	£1100	£1100

Fig. 74   A worked example of VAT account
(figures not included in main examples)

Debtors

Debtors is a technical term for money owed to the business at the date at which accounts are prepared. We have already dealt with VAT which may be owed. Other debtors will probably be sales.

They are invoices which have been raised during the period, but for which the money was not received until after the accounting date. These sales would not have appeared in the cash book because the cash book is a record of money actually received and spent, and the money will not have been received by the time accounts are prepared. As the money is owed to the business it is an asset. Therefore write the total sum involved against "debtors" under current assets on the draft balance sheet.

Because the sale was made in the year it will also affect the sales figure on the draft TPL and therefore the gross profit and net profit (or loss).

Add the amount owed to the sales figure and recalculate the profit figures – or loss figures. (Fig. 75). Obviously, the addition of sales will make a net profit bigger and a net loss smaller.

BALANCE SHEET

	£	£
Fixed assets		
Current assets		
Bank balance	150	
Debtors (example)	350	

TPL

Income	
Sales	19300
[*Add:* Debtors	350]
New sales total	£19650

Fig. 75 Amending TPL and balance sheet to include sales debtors (money owing)

Creditors

Creditors are people to whom the business owes money at the accounting date. In other words, purchases have been made, but money was not actually paid until after the end of the accounting period.

The most likely substantial creditor is a supplier of materials. The invoice for the goods will have been received before the end of the period, but money was not dispatched until after the accounting date, so the purchase does not appear in the cash book.

Examine the invoice file for any purchases which fall into this category and list them. Add them up to derive a total.

Once again, the inclusion of creditors will affect the TPL. If the creditor was for materials, add the amount owed to the total on the TPL. This will affect the gross profit and net profit or loss figures which should be erased and recalculated. (Fig. 76).

BALANCE SHEET

	£	£
Fixed assets		
Current assets		
Bank balance	150	
Debtors (example)	350	
Current liabilities		
Creditors (example)	150	

TPL

	£	£
Income		
Sales (including debtors)		19650
Less: Direct costs		
Purchases	6800	
[*Add:* Creditors	150]	
New purchases total	£6950	

Fig. 76 Amending TPL and balance sheet to include purchases creditor (money owed)

It is reasonable to ignore very small creditors among the overheads as they will be accounted for in the following period, but if a large bill is outstanding at the end of the year, it should be allowed for.

For example, perhaps only three out of four telephone bills have been paid within the accounting period. Obviously, the amount shown on the fourth bill will be outstanding.

Add the amount owing (a) to creditors on the balance sheet, (b) to the appropriate expenses heading on the profit and loss account, e.g. a telephone item would be added to the total opposite telephone costs, and so on.

Stock

At any one time, a business will have goods on the shelves which have not been sold, or work in progress. There may also be a range of materials and perhaps components which have not yet been used. These items are worth money as they will be sold or used eventually.

Because stock is worth something, and includes purchases which appear in the cash book, it should be accounted for.

Stock is valued at the lower of cost or value. In general, goods which are made up ready for sale can be valued at cost providing they are certain to be sold at a profit.

A business which holds stock which is worth a significant amount should hold a *stock take* on the day chosen to end the trading year.

Check thoroughly the contents of the stock and stores. All completed articles and batches of materials should be counted. Compile a list, make an estimate of the cost of each item, and add these to find the total value of stock held. This figure will be entered on the accounts.

Stock held is an asset, so its value is entered under current assets on the draft balance sheet.

Stock also represents materials purchased, but not yet used. Its value should therefore be entered on the TPL as a reduction in the costs of purchases.

Write this figure in beneath materials on the trading account and show the figure as a minus, to be subtracted from materials when calculating the gross profit. (Fig. 77).

BALANCE SHEET

	£	£
Fixed assets		
Current assets		
Bank balance	150	
Debtors	350	
Stock (example)	250	

TPL

	£	£
Income		
Sales		19650
Less: Direct costs		
Purchases	6950	
Less: Stock	(250)	
Sub-contract	1500	
		(8200)
Gross profit		£11450

Fig. 77   Amending balance sheet and TPL for stock

At this stage we are considering the preparation of accounts at the end of the first year or period. It is therefore unlikely that business was commenced with goods in stock. Purchases only become stock in an accounting sense at the end of the year. Dealing with opening stock in subsequent periods is dealt with on page 143.

Fixed assets

Fixed assets should be listed separately on a fixed asset

schedule. This will show the various categories of asset which were bought and sold. A rather more detailed approach is needed than was described in Chapter 5.

Our aim is to find the total value of fixed assets held by the business. This figure can then be entered on the balance sheet.

Draw up a draft schedule as shown in Fig. 78.

	DATE OF PUR- CHASE	DATE OF SALE	COST PRICE	SALE PRICE	PROFIT (LOSS) ON SALE OF ASSET	BALANCE
			£	£	£	£
Motor vehicles						
Car – Ford Escort XYZ 123 R	20 Oct.	—	1600	—	—	1600
Plant & Equipment						
Lathe	12 July	10 Mar.	500	(150)	(350)	—
Furniture & Fittings						
Workshop lighting	2 Mar.	—	400	—	—	400
			£2500	£(150)	£(350)	£2000

£2000 is then transferred as a balance to the balance sheet.

Fig. 78   An example of a Fixed Asset Schedule

The categories of asset – motor vehicles, equipment and furnishings are shown on the left. Opposite the description of the asset enter the value of the asset when bought, and the sale price, if any, if the asset was later resold. If the asset was not sold, leave the column blank.

These values can then be transferred to the balance

column on the right. If an asset was sold, subtract the sale price from the purchase price and record the difference as a profit or loss on sale of asset. This figure is then transferred to the TPL, being written in as a general overhead (Fig. 80). Note that a profit on sale would be a minus figure, as it represents less expense.

No balance will appear in the balance column of the fixed asset schedule as the entire value of the asset has been accounted for.

Add the entries in the balance column to derive a total.

Transfer the total to the draft balance sheet, opposite the heading fixed assets. There is no need to give a detailed description of the assets on the balance sheet.

Depreciation has already been mentioned. That is the rate at which an asset loses value with time. By convention depreciation is allowed for on accounts. While simple in concept, the calculations of depreciation can be a complex subject and an error in calculation is difficult to track down. It is not therefore a subject we will cover in this book.

The top portion of the balance sheet should now be complete. (Fig. 79).

	£	£
Fixed assets (from Schedule)		2000
Current assets		
Bank balance	150	
Debtors	350	
Stock	250	
		750
Total assets		2750
Less: Current liabilities		
Creditors		(150)
		£2600

Fig. 79   Assets and liabilities complete

We can now turn to the capital account, which appears on the same sheet.

Transferring the net profit or loss

The first step is to transfer the net profit or loss from the TPL. The examples given in this chapter were based on figures given in Fig. 40, page 82. Adjusted for debtors, creditors and stock, the trading and profit and loss account will now appear as in Fig. 80.

		£
Income		
Sales (including debtors)		19650
Less: Direct costs		
Opening stock	NIL	
Purchases (including creditors)	6950	
Less: Stock	(250)	
Sub-contract	1500	
		(8200)
Gross profit		11450
Less: General expenses		
Travel (75% × 1240)	930	
Rent of workshop	6000	
Heat and lighting	1300	
Postage and stationery	660	
Sundry items	300	
Loss on sale of lathe	350	
		(9540)
Net profit		£1910

Fig. 80   Amended TPL (from Fig. 40)

All amendments have now been made and if the calculations were made carefully, the figure shown should be accurate.

If a loss was made, the figure should be inserted as a minus

figure on the balance sheet. A profit is shown as a positive
entry. Fill in on the capital account as appropriate. (Fig. 81).

CAPITAL ACCOUNT

	£	£
Capital introduced (balance on cash account)		2870
Net profit (from TPL)		1910
		4780
Drawings		
Net loss (if applicable)	____	____

Fig. 81   Net profit (or loss) transferred from TPL

Capital introduced

Capital introduced is cash brought into the business from
private sources. This can mean a gift or possibly an injection
of money from private funds.

Either of these should have been recorded in the cash book
as they occurred, because they represent cash that has
actually been received.

Turn tc the receipts page of the cash book summary and
look at the "other income" column. Total such of these
entries as represent injections of money and transfer this
total to the capital account, as sundry income (private
money).

CAPITAL ACCOUNT

	£	£
Capital introduced:		
Possible negative balance on cash account		2870
Sundry income (private money)		1550
		4420

**Fig. 82   Transferring capital introduced from cash book
summary**

There is one other category of capital introduced, as mentioned on page 127. A negative balance on the cash account (i.e. more cash paid out than was received) shows that some of the proprietor's own money has been injected to pay for certain items. If the balance was positive, then it would not belong in capital introduced, but should be listed as a current asset. In our example, the balance on the cash account was negative and it is shown as a capital account item in Fig. 82.

Drawings

This heading represents all cash taken out of the business for private purposes such as living expenses.

Take the total given on the payments page of the cash book summary and transfer it to the balance sheet as shown (Fig. 83).

CAPITAL ACCOUNT

	£	£
Capital introduced:		
(2870 + 1550)		4420
Net profit (from TPL)		1910
		6330
Less:		
Drawings	3420	
Private proportion of car expenses	310	
		(3730)
		£2600

Fig. 83   Transferring drawings from cash book summary

There can be one other entry to add to drawings, and this is the private proportion of certain partial expenses.

Some expenses, such as car expenses, are split, part to the

business and part to private use. The private proportion of the total cost should go to drawings. In the case of our example in Fig. 40, page 82, motor expenses are split as follows:

Total car expenses	£1,240
75% to business use	¾ × 1,240 = 930
25% to drawings	¼ × 1,240 = 310
	£1,240

The figure of £310 would be entered on drawings on the capital account. (Fig. 83).

The capital account, and with it, the whole balance sheet, should now be completed.

Add the value of all current assets and extract a sub-total.

Do the same with current liabilities. If there is only one entry under this heading, regard that figure as a sub-total.

Add the fixed and current assets and, from the result, subtract the current liabilities.

The answer will be the overall difference between assets and liabilities. Underline the figure.

Now turn to the capital account. Should a profit have been made, add the capital introduced to the profit. Then subtract the drawings figure.

The result will represent the overall flow of cash into or out of the business during the year.

If a loss was made, add the loss to the drawings figure, and subtract this sum from capital introduced to give the difference.

If all calculations have been performed correctly, then the difference on the capital account should be the same as the difference between the value of the assets and liabilities belonging to the business. (Fig. 84).

Checking for errors

In the event that the two parts of the balance sheet do not balance, then a calculation has been performed wrongly.

Perhaps a cash book entry was not transferred properly.

Go back and check each step until the error is found.

There is no substitute for painstaking attention to detail when producing a set of accounts. The principles involved are straightforward. Any errors are caused by momentary lapses of attention.

To avoid the irritating task of tracking errors, try to perform each step of the procedure carefully, checking the accuracy of the results before moving on to the next stage.

Once the balance sheet has been completed and it agrees, the accounts are complete. They may then be typed neatly, together with a contents page and cover, and the pages photocopied. A signed declaration should be included (page 81).

	£	£
Fixed assets		2000
Current assets		
Bank balance	150	
Debtors	350	
Stock	250	
		750
Total assets		2750
Less: Current liabilities		
Creditors		(150)
		£2600
Capital account		
Capital introduced (2870 + 1550)		4420
Net profit		1910
		6330
Drawings (3420 + 310)		(3730)
		£2600

Fig. 84 The complete balance sheet and capital account

The accounts may then be submitted to the Inland Revenue for approval.

The new year

What has been said so far in this chapter relates to the first year or period of trading. The end of this period is the accounting date. However, business continues. As the new year begins, the cash book should still be maintained, with no gap left between the sets of records.

Once the initial trading period is over, you should draw up accounts at intervals of one year.

The cash book deals exclusively with cash flow in one period and has no relevance to the next year. The Tax Inspector may calculate certain factors relating to the fixed assets which are still possessed, using the fixed asset schedule. From the purely book-keeping point of view, no allowance need be made for the past once the new year has started.

The full set of accounts, on the other hand, will contain entries which should be taken into account when preparing accounts for the following year.

These entries are the balances shown on the balance sheet. A bank balance, for instance, does not disappear once the accounting date has passed. If it showed a credit balance, i.e. money in the bank, this sum will be available to the businessman in the next year.

It is vital therefore to ensure that these balances are transferred from the balance sheet to the new accounts.

How is this done?

All balances from the previous year's balance sheet are transferred to the current one, and added to the entries that will be made in the present period.

The balance sheet

Current assets and liabilities carry over into the next year as balances.

After the balance sheet is outlined, but before the current year's figures are transferred, enter all the balances from last

	£	£

Current assets
  Bank balance (already adjusted in bank
    reconciliation)
  Cash balance

                    old year

            +

                    new year

  VAT account (money owing)
  Already adjusted in VAT account
  summary
  Debtors: Transfer to relevant
  headings in TPL for new year

Liabilities
  Creditors: Transfer to relevant headings in TPL
    for new year
  VAT account if money owed. Balance in VAT
    account.

Capital account
  Opening capital (total in last year's capital
    account)
  Capital introduced (this year)
  Profit (this year)

  Drawings (this year)

  [Loss (this year)   ]

Fig. 85   Adding on the old year's balances

year's accounts. These are then used to adjust the entries for the current year.

Bank account

There is no need to physically add the closing bank account balance to the figure in the new year. This will be achieved anyway by producing a bank reconciliation.

When compiling a second or subsequent bank reconciliation the previous year's true balance may be entered as opening balance in the space shown in Fig. 69 (page 125). In the first year the balance would be nil.

Cash account

Any debit balance, or surplus, should be added to the current year's figure, because this much additional cash was available to the company at the beginning of the year.

A credit balance, or deficit, will have been entered as capital introduced in the previous year. As the balance on the capital account is transferred to the new capital account as opening capital, there is no need to add last year's deficit on the cash account as it will already have been done.

Stock

Opening stock, or the stock left over from the previous year is recorded as a positive figure on the TPL, above the entry marked "purchases". Note that this figure should be *added* to direct costs. The current year's stock figure is subtracted. (See Fig. 80, page 136).

VAT account

A balance on the VAT account (Fig. 73, page 128) will have been recorded on last year's balance sheet as a current asset or liability, depending on whether money was owed by or to the Customs and Excise.

The balance is incorporated . into the current year's account by adding it into the VAT account for the current year as an opening balance. If money is still owed to Customs and Excise, insert the opening balance in the *right*-hand column. If money is owed *by* Customs and Excise, add the balance into the *left*-hand column.

If this balance is taken into account, the new balance for the current year will be correct without further amendment.

Creditors and Debtors

Note that debtors and creditors are amounts owed and owing on profit and loss account items. They should *not* be added to debtors and creditors in the new year. Debtors should be *subtracted* from the sales figures in the next year. Creditors should be *added* into their appropriate expense headings in the next year. If creditors and debtors are not used to amend current TPL values then they will be counted twice, which will confuse the accounts.

Capital accounts

The capital account changes slightly in that it shows a new entry – *opening capital*. This is the balancing total on the previous year's accounts which is brought forward as the amount of capital available to the business in the new year. (Fig. 86).

CAPITAL ACCOUNT

	£	£
Opening capital		
Capital introduced		

Fig. 86   Entering the previous year's capital account balance

The fixed asset schedule

Like the capital account, the new fixed asset schedule should
show the balance brought forward for each category of asset.

A new column is therefore written into the schedule,
giving the opening balances. These are then added to the
costs of additions when calculating the balances (Fig. 87).

DATE OF PUR-CHASE	DATE OF SALE	OPENING BALANCE	COST PRICE	SALE PRICE	PROFIT/ (LOSS) ON SALE	BALANCE
Motor vehicles						
Plant & Equipment						
Furniture & Fittings						

**Fig. 87   Including opening balances in the Fixed Asset
Schedule**

Comparatives

It is interesting to be able to compare the performance of a
business in two different years. This can be achieved quite
simply by writing into a set of accounts the previous year's
figures.

This applies to the balance sheet and the trading and profit
and loss account, and can also be done to the statement of
income and expenditure.

When drafting the various pages of the accounts, write the
year in at the top so that it forms a heading. Write the
previous year to the right of it. The current year's figures
may have to shift to the left to make room.

After the current entries have been made and the accounts
checked, refer to the previous year's accounts and fill in all

the comparative figures. (Fig. 88). There is no calculation required in entering comparatives. They are purely an aid, enabling you to compare this year's figures with the last.

	CURRENT YEAR		PREVIOUS YEAR
	£	£	
Income			
Sales		19650	☐
Less: Direct costs			
Opening stock	☐		☐
Purchases	6950		☐
Less: Stock	(250)		☐
Sub-contract	1500		☐
		(8200)	☐
Gross profit		11450	☐
Less: General overheads			
Travel (75% × 1240)	930		☐
Rent of workshop	6000		
Heat and lighting	1300		☐
Postage and stationery	660		
Sundry items	300		☐
Loss on sale of lathe	350		☐
		(9540)	☐
Net profit		£1910	☐

Fig. 88 Writing comparatives into the TPL – the balance sheet may be amended similarly

What do you need to be a book-keeper?

Careful preparation and attention to detail are all the skills necessary to complete a full set of accounts, though you must remember that there are areas of accountancy which the amateur would be ill-advised to attempt. Allowance for depreciation, and the documentation of HP agreements and loan repayments have not been covered here, and reference should be made to advanced manuals or a professional book-keeper.

Flexibility is as essential to the preparation of your own accounts as it is to any other area of your life.

There is no need to despair at the thought of book-keeping. Much of it is straightforward. At the same time, do not over-reach yourself. This book has been deliberately formatted so that you may stop at any stage. You may only seek advice on keeping a cash book. The more ambitious will attempt complete accounts.

The level you reach will depend on your requirements or inclination.

A basic understanding of book-keeping will save you money, and time. It will give you a clearer insight into the day-to-day management of your business. Good luck!

Appendix:
Full set of accounts in finished form

JOHN B SMITH

T/A WEALDEN ART PRODUCTS

Trading and Profit and loss Account for the Year Ended 30th April 19XX

	19XX £	£
INCOME		
Sales		19,650
Less: Direct Costs		
Opening Stock	—	
Purchases	6950	
Less: Stock	(250)	
Subcontract	1500	
		(8200)
Gross Profit		11450
Less General Overheads		
Travel (75% × 1240)	930	
Rent of Workshop	6000	
Heat and lighting	1300	
Postage and stationery	660	
Sundry Items	300	
Loss on sale of Lathe	350	
		(9540)
Net Profit		1910

John B. Smith

T, A WEALDEN ART PRODUCTS

Balance Sheet as at 30th April 19XX

	19XX	
	£	£
Fixed Assets		2000
Current Assets		
Bank Balance	150	
Debtors	350	
Stock	250	
		750
Total Assets		2750
Less: Current Liabilities		
Creditors		(150)
		2600
Capital Account		
Capital Introduced (2870 + 1550)		4420
Net Profit		1910
		6330
Less: Drawings (3420 + 310)		(3730)
		2600

John B. Smith

T/A WEALDEN ART PRODUCTS

Fixed Asset Schedule at 30th April 19XX

	DATE OF PUR-CHASE	DATE OF SALE	COST PRICE	SALE PRICE	PROFIT/ (LOSS) ON SALE	BALANCE
MV Car. Ford Escort XYZ 123R	20 Oct.	—	1600	—	—	1600
P & E Lathe	12 July	10 Mar.	500	(150)	(350)	—
Furniture & Fittings Workshop Lighting	2 Mar.	—	400	—	—	400
			2500	(150)	(350)	2000

Index

IF YOU ARE STARTING YOUR OWN BUSINESS – YOU NEED

YOUR BUSINESS– THE RIGHT WAY TO RUN IT

by A. G. Elliot

Daily Mail '. . . his sometimes startling advice is worth reading . . .'

This book contains a huge amount of information needed by small business or self-employed.

Deals with subjects like: Short of cash? – Why are you in trouble? – Overdue accounts – Credit terms – Integrity – Tax – Chargeable expenses – VAT – PAYE – Legal aspects – Personnel – Interviewing – Staff training – Dismissal – References – Testimonials – Rate of profit – Stock control – Get your own publicity – Complaints – Glossary of business terms, phrases and abbreviations.

Uniform with this book

Elliot Right Way Books
BRIGHTON RD., LOWER KINGSWOOD, SURREY, U.K.

OUR PUBLISHING POLICY

HOW WE CHOOSE

Our policy is to consider every deserving manuscript and we can give special editorial help where an author is an authority on his subject but an inexperienced writer. We are rigorously selective in the choice of books we publish. We set the highest standards of editorial quality and accuracy. This means that a *Paperfront* is easy to understand and delightful to read. Where illustrations are necessary to convey points of detail, these are drawn up by a subject specialist artist from our panel.

HOW WE KEEP PRICES LOW

We aim for the big seller. This enables us to order enormous print runs and achieve the lowest price for you. Unfortunately, this means that you will not find in the *Paperfront* list any titles on obscure subjects of minority interest only. These could not be printed in large enough quantities to be sold for the low price at which we offer this series.

We sell almost all our *Paperfronts* at the same unit price. This saves a lot of fiddling about in our clerical departments and helps us to give you world-beating value. Under this system, the longer titles are offered at a price which we believe to be unmatched by any publisher in the world.

OUR DISTRIBUTION SYSTEM

Because of the competitive price, and the rapid turnover, *Paperfronts* are possibly the most profitable line a bookseller can handle. They are stocked by the best bookshops all over the world. It may be that your bookseller has run out of stock of a particular title. If so, he can order more from us at any time – we have a fine reputation for "same day" despatch, and we supply any order, however small (even a single copy), to any bookseller who has an account with us. We prefer you to buy from your bookseller, as this reminds him of the strong underlying public demand for *Paperfronts*. Members of the public who live in remote places, or who are housebound, or whose local bookseller is unco-operative, can order direct from us by post.

FREE

If you would like an up-to-date list of all paperfront titles currently available, send a stamped self-addressed envelope to
ELLIOT RIGHT WAY BOOKS, BRIGHTON RD.,
LOWER KINGSWOOD, SURREY, U.K.

PAPERFRONTS: The unique one-price series that proves the cheapest instructional books are often the best.